WORKING WITH

RISK

IN COUNSELLING
AND PSYCHOTHERAPY

Essential Issues in Counselling and Psychotherapy

Edited by Andrew Reeves

Counsellors and psychotherapists consider a number of important factors in their work with clients. Some are defined by training and theoretical orientation, some by context, and others by the client group with whom they work. However, across all these areas there are a number of essential issues – those that sit at the very core of practice – that must be considered by all therapists.

Essential Issues in Counselling and Psychotherapy is a series that brings together a number of new, accessible and practice-informed books that carefully and thoroughly address those considerations: the essential issues of practice that can challenge and shape all aspects of counselling and psychotherapy.

For new and forthcoming books in the series please visit www.uk.sagepub.com/cp

Assessment and Case Formulation in Counselling and Psychotherapy
Biljana van Rijn

The Therapeutic Relationship in Counselling and Psychotherapy
Rosanne Knox and Mick Cooper

Working with Risk in Counselling and Psychotherapy
Andrew Reeves

WORKING WITH

RISK

IN COUNSELLING
AND PSYCHOTHERAPY

BY
ANDREW REEVES

⑤SAGE

Los Angeles | London | New Delhi
Singapore | Washington DC

⑨SAGE

Los Angeles | London | New Delhi
Singapore | Washington DC

SAGE Publications Ltd
1 Oliver's Yard
55 City Road
London EC1Y 1SP

SAGE Publications Inc.
2455 Teller Road
Thousand Oaks, California 91320

SAGE Publications India Pvt Ltd
B 1/I 1 Mohan Cooperative Industrial Area
Mathura Road
New Delhi 110 044

SAGE Publications Asia-Pacific Pte Ltd
3 Church Street
#10-04 Samsung Hub
Singapore 049483

© Andrew Reeves 2015

First published 2015

Editor: Kate Wharton
Assistant editor: Laura Walmsley
Production editor: Rachel Burrows
Copyeditor: Sophie Richmond
Proofreader: Danielle Ray
Indexer: Bill Farrington
Marketing manager: Camille Richmond
Cover design: Lisa Harper-Wells
Typeset by: C&M Digitals (P) Ltd, Chennai, India

Library of Congress Control Number: 2014942359

British Library Cataloguing in Publication data

A catalogue record for this book is available from
the British Library

ISBN 978-1-4462-7290-9
ISBN 978-1-4462-7291-6 (pbk)

For Diane, Adam, Katie and Emily for their
unconditional patience.

To ... Rita and Emily for their
unconditional support

CONTENTS

ABOUT THE AUTHOR

Andrew Reeves has worked as a social worker and then as a therapist for over 25 years. His previous books include: *Key Issues for Counselling in Action: Second Edition* (Sage, 2008 – co-edited with Windy Dryden); *Counselling Suicidal Clients* (Sage, 2010); *An Introduction to Counselling and Psychotherapy: From Theory to Practice* (Sage, 2013); *Challenges in Counselling: Self-Harm* (Hodder Education, 2013); and *The Handbook of Individual Therapy: Sixth Edition* (Sage, 2014 – co-edited with Windy Dryden). He has produced (with Jon Shears and Sue Wheeler) an award-winning training DVD, *Tight Ropes and Safety Nets: Counselling Suicidal Clients*, and was Lead Author for the Counselling MindEd project. He is a former Editor of *Counselling and Psychotherapy Research* journal.

ACKNOWLEDGEMENTS

I would like to thank Kate Wharton, Susannah Trefgarne, Laura Walmsley, Rachel Burrows and the full team at Sage for their unstinting support and encouragement throughout the writing process.

INTRODUCTION

Chapter outline

This introductory chapter presents a context for the exploration of risk in counselling and psychotherapy. It presents risk as an integral part of the therapeutic process that is deserving of attention and exploration and then frames it as a relational process, as well as a factor that is worthy of a more discrete consideration. The importance of contracting is discussed in which the nature and form of risk, as well as therapist response to risk situations, can be explored. The chapter will then consider how the book is structured, offering a brief overview of each chapter and how they relate to practice.

BEGINNINGS

When we begin training as counsellors and psychotherapists we are often focused on all the good that can come out of successful therapy. After all, what is there not to like? People who are experiencing levels of distress or unhappiness come along to speak confidentially with a caring and compassionate therapist, and then feel better. Simply put. We know that things are typically much more complex than that, but the compelling nature of therapy has, in the early days at least, the potential to obscure the important realities of the therapeutic process. That is not to say that there isn't any truth in the optimism of the beginning trainee, but that as training progresses it is not untypical for trainees to go through a period of disillusionment as the contractual, ethical and professional responsibilities of being a therapist become clearer.

We are introduced to the concepts of ethics, law, social policy, procedural demands, as well as boundaries, contracting, challenge, and so on. Suddenly, the focus seems to move away from the beauty of the relational process, and instead shines a light on the 'workings out': those things that are actually integral to the therapeutic process and contribute to it being a safe and appropriate space. It is a bit like taking a watch apart: taken as a whole the watch represents an amazing synchronicity of a multitude of constituent parts working together seamlessly, the complexity mostly hidden. Take the back off the watch and begin to remove the dial, face, hands, winding mechanism, etc. and it quickly becomes obvious that each part, no matter how tiny and seemingly irrelevant, plays an integral role in the dynamic process of telling the time. Therapy for me is very much like that: the sitting together and talking with a client belies the complexity of the process that is actually taking place and each part of that process, no matter how tiny or seemingly irrelevant, has an integral role in the nature of the relationship and its outcome. So while the optimism of the beginning trainee is important and accurate (people do actually feel better because of going to see a counsellor or psychotherapist), the 'small print' as well as the 'headline' needs to be taken into consideration.

THE NATURE OF RISK

It is therefore at this stage, and in this context, that I would like to introduce the concept of risk, which is the focus of this book. For much of the time in therapy risk might be considered to be one of those tiny and seemingly irrelevant parts of therapy that has little to do with the overall experience of it, sort of ticking away in the background but not particularly significant in the process. And yet when we really think about therapy and stand back from the detail, risk is a significant feature from the very beginning: consider Alex below.

Alex

Alex is a 32-year-old man. He works as an advertising executive and, until six months ago, was in a happy relationship with his partner. This relationship was very important to Alex. He grew up in care, his mother having died when he was 11 years old and without him ever knowing his father. He has no siblings and no other extended family. While there have been lots of friendships, most have turned out to be transient and unreliable. When Alex met Susie he was 19 years old and she was 22. Alex felt that they were close, happy, honest and connected. As such, Alex felt an unbearable devastation when he came home one afternoon four months previously to find Susie dead. She had taken an overdose and left a suicide note apologising to Alex, saying it wasn't his fault. Alex seeks out and makes contact with a counsellor.

Alex's situation is both shocking and distressing. With little support and a background of uncertain care and love, he has found himself in a situation unexpectedly that challenges the security and stability of his whole life. Risk is layered throughout Alex's situation and it is important for his counsellor to be mindful of this dynamic when meeting him for the first time. Risks in this situation include:

- Unexpected death of partner through suicide
- Traumatic bereavement and possibly lots of unanswered questions
- Little social support
- Death of mother when very young, resulting in Alex being placed in care
- No relationship with father
- Alex's own risk factors, including age, being male, bereavement, social isolation, uncertain attachments when young, etc.
- Alex's suicide potential
- Taking the step of speaking with a counsellor (confidentiality, shame, fear of being let down again).

Looking at risk in this way we can begin to move away from perhaps a binary understanding of risk (that there is risk present or there isn't), and instead consider risk as a multi-dimensional process, which incorporates states of being and shades of uncertainty. Risk is arguably an inevitable aspect of living and is contextually defined through our social, relational, cultural and demographic identity. Risk is perhaps always present in our lives and our choices and decisions in many ways centre around our capacity and willingness to negotiate risks: taking them, avoiding them, or finding ways of mitigating them so that they are reduced. We are in a constant process of being at risk in different ways and at different times.

We can apply this binary vs multi-dimensional understanding of risk to Alex's situation too. Do we see Alex as someone whose risk has to be assessed and managed in counselling, or explored, or seen as part of his existential struggle, or mitigated, or as something to be fearful of, or energised by? Is risk inherent in who Alex is, or rather is it part of his everyday living – a thread that runs through his entire life that has simply become apparent through crisis? It is an interesting philosophical position to consider. My own professional background has included working for many years in adult mental health crisis services and my learning from that experience is that we are all but one heartbeat away from a crisis. Crises ultimately have to be negotiated and the associated risks faced, if we are able to do it.

Pause for reflection

1 Think of your own life currently. What are the risks embedded in your life?
2 How do these embedded risks differ from situational risks (that arise from a particular situation or circumstance)?
3 What is your relationship to the risks in your life (e.g. do you fear them, feel empowered by them, try to mitigate them, or seek them out)?
4 How might this shape who you are and your view of the world?

THERAPY AND RISK

In working with a multi-dimensional view of risk, which is my intention throughout this book, we need to pay careful consideration to the implications of that for the counsellor and psychotherapist. If we take Alex again: risk permeates Alex's situation and what he brings to his counsellor and, in many ways, Alex will need to explore and consider those risks as part of a process of change. However, Alex has sought out counselling perhaps because of the risks he identifies and, in doing so, is either consciously or unconsciously looking for something from his counsellor perhaps because he feels chaotic and uncontained. In response to his feelings he might want stability, security, predictability and perhaps containment. In other words, Alex does not need his counsellor to be as chaotic and uncontained as he might feel as that might only exacerbate his sense of crisis.

The task for us as therapists, therefore, is to find ways of achieving a careful balance: to enable sufficient space and movement in the therapeutic relationship to allow for risk (for that is where important exploration may take place), while offering sufficient containment and boundaries to help ensure the risk is not overwhelming or a threat to either the client or the therapist. Alex must be afforded the confidential and respectful space to engage with and explore his feelings about Susie's death, in the context of his own childhood experiences, while at the same time he must be contained and held securely by appropriate boundaries. It is not an easy balance to achieve and many factors can tip the balance unhelpfully, including poor boundaries, lack of attention to boundaries, personally held views on the part of the therapist, anxiety and fear, and procedural demands inconsistent with the ethos and philosophy of therapy. These will all be explored further in later chapters.

PARAMETERS AND CONTRACTING

In thinking about containment and safety, counselling contracts help set parameters and expectations, as well as identifying and clarifying boundaries (Sills, 2006). Sills (2006: 5) states that, 'the therapeutic relationship, with its inevitable power imbalance and its capacity to arouse very deep and disturbing issues, is in particular need of structure and order to contain it. The contract helps to provide this structure.' I have previously outlined a number of reasons for contracting (Reeves, 2013b: 255). It:

- Helps clarify both practitioner's and client's rights and responsibilities
- Helps clarify the responsibilities (and rights) of the organisation (where therapy is provided by an organisation rather than an independent practitioner)
- Respects the client's autonomy
- Helps ensure that clients make an informed choice about entering into therapy
- Clarifies practical considerations, (e.g. fees, timings of sessions, venue, length of each session, number of sessions offered, implications for cancelled or missed sessions, endings, etc.)
- Helps set boundaries, such as confidentiality
- Helps the therapist reflect on their own competence to offer therapy to the client, given the client's needs and expectations
- Helps contain the process of therapy, which might be difficult or distressing for the client.

While some of the points above seem more procedural than relational (such as practical considerations), they are vitally important for the safety and security of the client. They all relate to mutual expectations of each other that are vital in the establishment of trust. For example, it may well have been for Alex growing up in care that the practical boundaries were not always apparent: who represented the parent; what Alex might be able to expect from others; how long he might stay in any particular care home or foster placement; when his social worker might leave and be replaced by another. For Alex to know that his counsellor had taken the time and consideration to think about and make clear these issues might be the first important step in Alex being able to trust them.

I will refer to the contracting process throughout this book, paralleling perhaps how it should happen in therapy too. That is, not talked about right at the beginning and never mentioned again, but rather an important thread that runs through the therapeutic process and that can contribute to a sense of consistency and wholeness – as it will run through this book, holding the chapters and overall narrative together.

THE STRUCTURE OF THE BOOK

Early on I have tried to begin to name some philosophical parameters that are likely to underpin my writing about risk: that risk is an inevitable part of living; life is often typified by the relationship we have with risk; risk will inevitably and always be part of the client's presentation; and that working with risk in counselling and psychotherapy is an important therapeutic process rather than something simply to be managed and responded to. Our first stopping point after this introduction in Chapter 2, 'What Do We Mean by Risk?', looks at definitions and thinks about some of the issues raised here in a bit more detail. We will consider some legal and ethical parameters, but will also look at the importance of risk therapeutically.

In Chapter 3, 'Risk Assessment: Talking and Ticking Boxes', we will take the idea of risk as part of a therapeutic process and critically reflect on this in the light of current practice and its apparent evidence base. More specifically, we will explore the idea of risk assessment being a particular thing that we should do, and reflect on ways in which we might do it. The wider concepts around assessment and case formulation are more fully explored by van Rijn (2015), but here we will think specifically about risk and how the ticking of boxes (through the use of risk tools and questionnaires) sits alongside a dialogic approach to risk (where the exploration is embedded in the therapeutic narrative).

Chapters 4 ('Working with a Risk of Suicide'), 5 ('Working with Self-Injury and Self-Harm'), 6 ('The Danger of Violence and Harm to Others'), 7 ('Safeguarding and Child Protection') and 8 ('Mental Health Crisis: Danger and Opportunity') will all look at particular aspects of risk that present most commonly in counselling and psychotherapy. From the risk of suicide and self-harm and violence to others, through to child protection and mental health crisis, we need to be mindful of both the therapeutic process and our responsibilities to our clients, as outlined in the contracts we have agreed and any procedures within which we work.

Chapter 9, 'Using Supervision to Manage Risks in the Therapeutic Process' looks at particular issues that might be present in the therapeutic relationship, including crossed boundaries (e.g. sexual, financial), exploitation of clients, lack of ethical thinking, as well as risks to us as therapists, such as poor self-care, burnout and vicarious trauma, and the role of supervision and other strategies in supporting us with these.

Chapter 10, 'Positive Risk-Taking', takes the starting philosophy outlined in this introductory chapter that risk is an important therapeutic process that can provide the opportunity for change, and develops it further. Here we will consider the concept of positive risk-taking. That is, working proactively and collaboratively with clients around particular risks and helping them to take responsibility for their own wellbeing and safety, where possible and appropriate. In many ways all counselling and psychotherapy is about positive risk-taking in that we actively work with risk all the time, but there are ways in which we can do that more specifically and interventions we might use to help support that process. Finally, Chapter 11 will work to bring the points made throughout the chapters together into a coherent framework for good practice.

A QUESTION OF MODALITY

My aim here is to write a book that is generally non-modality specific but more integrative of a number of ideas from practice. I must confess to an attraction to the idea from research that good outcomes tend to be linked more with the quality of the relationship than a particular intervention strategy (Gaston et al., 1998; Hovarth and Bedi, 2002). With that in mind, it is my intention to try to write in an inclusive way. My hope here is that, rather than articulating a specific model for what I consider to be good practice I will, instead, provide a number of ideas for readers to critically engage with. It will then be up to you to consider ways in which you might integrate those ideas you like and agree with in your work, and abandon freely anything else I might have written that you consider rubbish. I hope not to write much rubbish, but it is a sad realisation I have had to address during my life that I am not always right. But don't tell anyone I said that.

AND FINALLY ... COUNSELLING OR PSYCHOTHERAPY?

It is always a challenge for anyone sitting down to write a book about counselling and psychotherapy to think about which terminology to use. Spinelli (2006: 38) writes that: 'Some have suggested that the main distinction between psychotherapy and counselling is that while the former requires clients to recline on a couch, the latter only provides an armchair.' Even in this playful attempt to consider differences there are challenges, in that most psychotherapists will provide a chair as well! I have discussed elsewhere (Reeves, 2013b) what I consider to be the differences and similarities between the two terms, accepting that some will see clear differences and others no difference at all. For the purposes of this book I would like to repeat what I have said previously, that I will refer to 'counsellors' and 'psychotherapists' and 'counselling' and 'psychotherapy' to acknowledge that, regardless of the actuality of the situation, people define themselves using these terms. I will also use terms like 'therapy', 'therapist' and 'practitioner' for example, simply to facilitate the flow of text.

Chapter summary

In this introductory chapter we have considered a number of aspects of risk and how we think about risk as a working concept. More specifically, we have seen that risk is an everyday feature of all our lives, in some shape or form, and that our challenge is to find proactive and positive ways of engaging with it. Within the context of therapy specifically, risk is often seen as a binary concept – that risk either exists or it does not – rather than risk being present for clients in a multi-dimensional way. As such, it is helpful to think of risk as an important aspect of therapy that, with care and attention, can provide a fertile space for clients to explore the issues that have brought them to therapy and consider key points of change and insight. That is, risk can positively be worked with rather than simply be something we think has to be managed away. Finally, we have considered the overall structure of the book and the different types of risk that we might encounter in our work.

2

WHAT DO WE MEAN BY RISK?

Chapter outline

This chapter will consider definitions of risk informed by the general usage of the term, but also how we might understand risk in the context of the therapeutic process. We will look at how risk is typically perceived as a possibility of danger, but we will also look at the opportunities that can be inherent in risk for therapeutic insight and change and set a conceptual understanding for later chapters in the book.

INTRODUCTION

It is surprising when you begin to read around the concept of risk how little attention is actually given in the literature to defining it. It seems to be a word whose meaning we take for granted, without ever really digging beneath the surface. Risk is about danger, of things going wrong – why look any further than that? Yet the reality is that much is to be achieved by looking at the term in a little more depth if we are to provide a useful context within which we can consider practice implications. That is, as counsellors and psychotherapists we need to really understand what we mean by risk and all its implications if we are to work effectively with clients in responding to it. Simply defining the term, however, does not necessarily make life much easier because we then need to think about the implications of the definition, such as risk of what, to whom, how, and whether our task in working with risk is about managing it, mitigating its likelihood, or using it as a potential opportunity for change and growth, or all of these at different times. The bottom line here is whether risk is necessarily bad and should be avoided or whether, in a transparent collaboration with our clients, we should embrace risk as an inevitable consequence of living and see in it real opportunities that might not be afforded without it.

DEFINING OUR TERMS

A generic definition of risk can be found in the Oxford English Dictionary (*Oxford English Dictionary*, 2014), which offers a number of working definitions. Risk is:

> (Exposure to) the possibility of loss, injury, or other adverse or unwelcome circumstance; a chance or situation involving such a possibility [or]
>
> To act in such a way as to bring about the possibility of (an unpleasant or unwelcome event) [or]
>
> to take a risk, be bold or daring.

Risk is defined by context, in that if I were writing a text on financial matters then risk would be applied specifically to financial outcome, or a book on architecture would consider risk in building design, or perhaps the risk of spread of disease if I were writing about epidemiology. Each context would bring a different nuance to our understanding of risk. In our context we are talking about risk in counselling and psychotherapy. That, in itself, is not straightforward because risk might be positioned on the part of the client (e.g. risk of suicide), the organisation (e.g. risk from procedure or policy), or the practitioner (e.g. risk of harm from the client). However, if we take the three definitions outlined above we can see some key characteristics:

- Risk is about being exposed to danger or uncertainty, or the possibility of this.
- The possibility of risk can be brought about by our actions.
- Risk is not always about danger, but can be associated with being bold or daring.

Here we can see that risk might emerge because of actions, or potential actions, or might be a consequence of an exposure to certain circumstances, and that it does not necessarily equate to danger. This latter point, outlined in the third definition above, is helpful in that it opens the opportunity to working with risk rather than simply avoiding it. In the context of our own work we, or our clients, might be supported to be bold or daring and, in doing so, make changes. One example of this would be working with someone who self-injures to cope with overwhelming feelings. The temptation would be to act to avoid such risk, whereas being bold might equate to working proactively with the self-injuring process to enable the client to gain insight and find new ways for self-support.

As practitioners we might need to reflect on whether we are essentially risk averse in our life or risk proactive. By risk averse I mean behaving or thinking in a way that avoids or mitigates risk at most opportunities, whereas by risk proactive I mean engaging with the possibility of risk with a view to the potential for a good outcome. This is typically not a binary state – that we are risk averse or risk proactive – but rather we might find that we respond to different kinds of risks at different points or time. Our capacity to tolerate risk might also be influenced by a number of factors. If I take myself for example: in some situations I would be risk proactive, such as in some sports or physical activities, whereas in others I might be risk averse, such as investments and financial matters. My relationship with risk is not a static entity, but one that fluctuates depending on the nature or context of the risk, or at different points in my life.

Pause for reflection

1 Consider your relationship with risk in response to the following situations: financial matters; driving; sports or other physical activities; culture and media; and relationships.
2 Notice whether your relationship to risk changes in different contexts, or is static throughout.
3 Thinking about relationships, what factors either support you to take risks in relationships, or be risk averse?

Like many aspects of counselling and psychotherapy, the starting point is often in our own reflections and insights. The more we are able to understand ourselves the more we can connect with our client's frame of reference or perspective (Adams, 2013). The same is true for risk. The more we can understand our own attitudes and responses to risk the more we will be able to transfer that into the therapeutic relationship and help our clients understand their own relationship to risk and, in doing so, help them also to think about responsibility. This is an interesting point because working with risk is also about working with personal responsibility. It is my assertion for example, that we are *responsible to* our clients, rather than *responsible for* our clients. Unless a client temporarily or permanently lacks capacity to make informed decisions for themselves (perhaps because of age, high levels of distress, such as psychosis, or an organic disorder), the work of therapy is ultimately about working with the client's capacity and willingness to take responsibility for their own lives. This raises interesting philosophical questions about the balance of responsibility in the therapeutic process when risk is present. Consider Alisha below.

Alisha

Alisha is 18 years old and has experienced depression for five years. During that time she has self-injured, cutting her arms, and has struggled with some suicidal thoughts. She has a supportive family but is generally reluctant to tell them too much about how she feels as she does not want them to worry about her. Her General Practitioner (GP), who is also aware of Alisha's potential suicidality, has prescribed her anti-depressants. She has talked about her suicidal feelings in counselling. In a session she says that her suicidal feelings have become stronger and that she has started to think more specifically about the types of things she might do. However, she does not want this to be shared with her GP as she thinks she will be okay and will probably be able to manage the suicidal thoughts on her own while also continuing to explore them in counselling.

This is not an uncommon presentation in therapy, where a client talks about their suicidal feelings but is reluctant to disclose this to others. The risk in this situation is informed by:

- Research evidence around suicide risk (risk factors, such as Alisha's age, that she has a history of self-injury, is depressed, is on anti-depressants, and has suicidal ideation moving to intent) (Reeves, 2010)
- The form and nature of any protective factors, such as the quality of the therapeutic alliance and the availability of support outside therapy
- The context of therapy and the organisation's policy around suicide risk
- The contract agreed between Alisha and her counsellor, specifically around the limitations of confidentiality
- Alisha's capacity and willingness to support herself at higher-risk times
- The therapist's capacity and willingness to work with suicide risk.

We will explore these issues in more detail in Chapter 4, when we look more specifically at working with suicide risk, but Alisha's situation illustrates the complexity of working with risk and the importance of the therapist's capacity and willingness to tolerate risk.

RISK IN CONTEXT

In thinking about the complexity of working in counselling and psychotherapy in relation to risk it is helpful to break down the definition and consider it in different contexts. I suggest five contexts of thinking about risk, which are:

- *Situational*: risks that relate to specific potential events or situations
- *Relational*: risks that emerge in the therapeutic relationship
- *Contextual*: risks that relate to the context in which therapy takes place
- *Professional*: risks that relate to professional behaviour or action
- *Personal*: risks to the wellbeing of the practitioner.

Situational risks

Situational risks are those most often thought about when we think about risk as it presents in counselling and psychotherapy. They relate to specific events or situations, or their potential. It is situational risks that are most commonly specifically referred to when contracting with a client, and can include:

- Potential for client suicide
- Self-injury and self-harm
- Safeguarding concerns
- Child protection
- Risk of violence to others
- Terrorist threat.

If we consider the short vignette about Jason:

Jason

Jason is 13 years of age and has been attending his school counselling for several weeks; his Year Head referred him following untypical

(Continued)

(Continued)

aggressive outbursts in class. Jason has been reluctant to talk to teaching staff about his worries, but was willing to see a counsellor in school. The counselling relationship has developed well. However, Jason arrives for a session with bruising to his face. His counsellor asks about the bruising and Jason says it was caused during a fight. The counsellor is not convinced this is the case and, on questioning Jason further, it is implied that his father caused the bruising during an 'incident' at home.

Safeguarding concerns are important considerations for therapists working with children, young people and vulnerable adults. In this scenario, the counsellor is faced with strong suspicions that Jason might have suffered (and potentially be suffering in an ongoing way) physical abuse by his father. The situational risk here relates to safeguarding and child protection concerns and the circumstances at home that may indicate physical abuse. This is typical of a situational risk where an external circumstance or specific client presentation indicates risk, usually of harm to the client or another person.

Pause for reflection

1 Think about the clients you see and identify the key situational risks that might arise.
2 How would you respond to such situational risks and what mechanisms have you put in place to support yourself with them?

Relational risks

Relational risks are those that are embedded in the therapeutic relationship and are typically representative of some dynamic between client and therapist. Sometimes they may be very apparent and obvious, while at other times might emerge slowly without being noticed early on. This is where therapist self-reflection (the internal supervisor) and formal supervision can be invaluable, in identifying areas of concern before harm is caused. Relational risks might include:

- Sexual attraction
- Financial mismanagement or inappropriate interaction
- Unacknowledged or mismanaged transference issues
- Unacknowledged or mismanaged countertransference issues
- Actions that lead to shame or deplete the client's autonomy or wellbeing, such as anger or false accusation.

If we take the first point here and consider the vignette about Diane:

Diane

Diane is 28 years old and has sought out independent counselling because of confusion around her sexuality. She looked for a therapy service that offered support around sexuality and asked for a female counsellor. She has found the counsellor to be non-judgemental, empathic, warm and compassionate. As the sessions have progressed Diane has noticed sexual feelings towards her counsellor. She understands that these are not likely to be reciprocated, but she has become flirty. The counsellor has not identified Diane's feelings and has interpreted them simply as responsive and friendly, and has responded in a similar way. Diane wonders whether perhaps her counsellor does have deeper feelings for her after all.

Sexual feelings can occur in therapy, either experienced by the client for their counsellor, or vice versa. Such feelings are in and of themselves unsurprising, given that therapy is essentially about two people (or more, if in a group scenario) engaging in a relationship partly characterised by empathy and intimacy. With good supervision such feelings can be worked with effectively and their meaning explored without harm to either party. Such dynamics between a client and a therapist that are to do with their relationship can be understood as relational risks. In the situation with Diane these have not been recognised and, while the counsellor has not specifically encouraged these feelings, her actions – through lack of insight rather than malice – have increased the risk of a potential transgression of boundaries and harm for Diane. There is an important difference here between risk caused through naivety and intent: the latter being deliberate and intentional exploitation of a client, such as seeking out a sexual relationship or financial gain.

Pause for reflection

1   What relational risks have you encountered in your work with clients?
2   Are there any common factors that you can identify, e.g. type of client, working setting?
3   What support do you have in place so that you can become aware of them as soon as possible?

Contextual risks

Contextual risks are those that relate to the context in which therapy is delivered, and can arise because of a number of factors in the delivery of counselling. Organisations that deliver counselling, or practitioners who move into independent practice, all have a responsibility to ensure that the delivery of therapy is ethical, safe, accessible and appropriate. Contextual risks might include:

- Inconsistent or inequitable delivery of services
- Lack of clear ethical position in relation to the therapy offered
- Inconsistent expectations of practitioners working in the setting
- Lack of thought or consideration by a practitioner working independently around procedures or working practices
- Procedures or policies inconsistent either with an understood philosophical base for counselling, or with understood ethical positions.

If we take issues surrounding independent practice we can consider them in relation to the vignette about Michael.

Michael

Michael is a counsellor who qualified six months ago. He has found it difficult to secure paid work as a therapist and has decided to establish an independent practice. He uses a room at home and has designed a basic website, giving potential clients information about him, the services he offers and his fees. Michael has been seeing Rory, who is 18 years old. Rory has a history of depression and has never had counselling previously. During a session Rory tells Michael that he feels suicidal and during the last week has done some research about the most effective method of killing himself; that is his intention. Michael realises that Rory needs urgent assessment and support and obtains Rory's consent. However, when he asks Rory cannot remember who his GP is, and Michael does not know what services exist locally, or how to contact them.

This is sadly not an unusual situation: therapists increasingly look towards independent practice as a mechanism of supporting themselves financially very soon after qualifying, without giving sufficient thought to the things that need to be in place to support practice (that might be more obvious in an organisational setting, such as consultation, etc.). In this instance Michael has failed to undertake the most basic research about what crisis services exist, who can access them, or how. Additionally, Michael has also failed to take sufficient referral information about other support, such as Rory's GP, and even though he has contracted to inform others if concerned about a client's immediate safety; he does not have the information to do so when it is needed. The risk here is that Rory has disclosed difficult and personal information to Michael hoping (either consciously or unconsciously) that Michael will contain his distress and support him, but is then uncertain about what help he will actually receive.

Pause for reflection

1 What settings do you work in and what are the particular contextual risks you think might present?
2 What steps could you take now to mitigate these risks, e.g. researching key information, challenging policy that concerns you?

Professional risks

As therapists we have a duty to our clients to safeguard their wellbeing during therapy itself, but also prior to therapy commencing and after the therapy has finished. Additionally, our own behaviour can have far-reaching consequences for our professional integrity, but also for the validity of the therapeutic relationship itself. Actions that seem to be unrelated to our work as therapists can bridge back into our professional roles very quickly. Consider the scenario about Sandie.

Sandie

Sandie is a therapist who works for an alcohol and drug agency. She has been working there for some years and has established a good reputation for herself as a challenging but empathic therapist who is very effective with clients. It is the nature of her challenge, particularly around the clients' use of alcohol and drugs, that is most respected by people who go to see her. Sandie has experienced some personal problems and, following a difficult time, was stopped by the police and charged with drink driving. Her case was heard in court and the local newspaper published a story about her, which received a lot of local attention given her professional role. Several of her clients have ended their therapy with her saying that they no longer trust her, feel let down by her and 'cannot accept challenge from a hypocrite'.

Whatever your own thoughts about the rights and wrongs of the decisions made by Sandie's clients, or about her behaviour in her personal life, the consequences for her therapy practice and for her clients are real. The risk here is that Sandie has lost both professional standing locally but also the trust of some of her clients. They feel let down by her and do not consider her challenge around their own drinking to be valid and authentic. As therapists we need to keep in mind the consequences of our actions even if they do not appear to be related to our work as therapists. Our presence on and use of social media applications is a case in point here, with research indicating how little attention we give to the consequences of our actions on our work as therapists by what we might post, thinking these are private postings but never having paid attention to our privacy settings (Tunick, Mednick and Conroy, 2011; Barker, 2013). New opportunities for the development of professional risks are emerging all the time.

Pause for reflection

1 Can you identify other professional risks, either that you have encountered in others or can identify in your own actions?
2 What steps do you take to minimise the potential for such professional risks, such as discussion in supervision, etc.?

Personal risks

Finally we need to think about the personal risks that might be present as a consequence of our work as a therapist. These typically centre on the impact of our work and how we attend to our own needs. While effective self-care is an ethical requirement, it is not uncommon for therapists either not to think about this explicitly at all, or not to have a systematic mechanism for when they can look after themselves. Personal risks can include:

- Vicarious trauma
- Burnout
- Relationship or family difficulties
- Bringing personal material into client work
- Inappropriate self-disclosure
- Meeting own needs in therapy rather than those of the client.

The insidious nature of personal risks can mean that the negative consequences can be present long before we are aware of them, thus minimising the effectiveness of any subsequent action we may take, particularly if the therapist does not have adequate or regular mechanisms for checking out their own wellbeing. Consider the scenario about Khalida.

Khalida

Khalida is a busy therapist who works in two agencies and also has a private practice. One agency deals with post-trauma and Khalida often supports clients who have experienced profoundly distressing events. She is a very effective therapist and ensures that she has good quality supervision in place. However, she does find it difficult to set her own limits, particularly around workload, and as a consequence sees a lot of clients in the week. When she gets home she has little time for family and friends. The relationship with her partner has been typified by increasing tension and arguments, and Khalida feels that she has emotionally withdrawn from the home situation. Her partner accuses Khalida of caring for her clients more than she does her family.

The phenomenon and impact of 'compassion fatigue' (Craig and Sprang, 2010) might be familiar to many therapists: arriving home and not wanting to hear any more problems, including those of family and friends; rather, just putting on the television and taking personal space. Repeated over time this can become a disengaging pattern that can have negative consequences for relationships, for example. Such personal risks are important to keep in mind as they can be experienced not only by the therapist themselves but also by those around them. Failure to meet personal needs can diminish our efficacy as a therapist and impact on our clients as well.

We can see the broad nature of risk through how different risks can present in many different ways. I hope I have illustrated here that while situational risks, such as risk of client suicide, are clearly very important and are often the first thing we think about when asked about risk, other risks too require equivalent attention to safeguard the wellbeing of the client and ourselves.

Chapter summary

In this chapter we have looked at definitions of risk and highlighted the importance of seeing risk not only as having the potential for a negative outcome but also a state in which we and our clients can be bold or daring with a view to a positive outcome or change. The nature of risk can be positioned differently, depending on how it relates to the client, the therapist or the context in which therapy takes place. I have suggested five types of risks that counsellors and psychotherapists can effectively consider: situational risks, which relate to particular issues therapists might experience, such as risk of suicide; relational risks, which concern aspects of the relationship that might result in harm if not addressed, such as sexual feelings or other compromised boundaries; contextual risks, which relate to the context of therapy, such as poorly drafted policy and inequitable service provision; professional risks, which relate to the behaviour or actions of the therapist that might impact negatively on client work; and personal risks, which relate to practitioner self-care and wellbeing.

3

RISK ASSESSMENT: TALKING AND TICKING BOXES

Chapter outline

'Risk assessment' is increasingly used as a term to describe a particularly one-dimensional activity: that is, an assessment of the nature, degree or extent of harm that an individual might encounter. This chapter challenges the idea of 'risk assessment' as an activity isolated from other relational factors, and instead argues that it is inextricably linked with other social, psychological and relational mechanisms. The use of risk questionnaires and assessment tools will be explored and discussed, as will how risk in its widest sense can be incorporated into the therapeutic dialogue.

INTRODUCTION

The term 'risk assessment' is one that has increasingly come into health, social and psychological parlance. Psychiatrists do it, social workers do it, teachers do it, therapists do it; it is now a shared activity with each professional group bringing their own particular perspective and ideas. In Chapter 2 we looked at definitions of risk: if we revisit one of those definitions from the *Oxford English Dictionary* (2014):

(Exposure to) the possibility of loss, injury, or other adverse or unwelcome circumstance; a chance or situation involving such a possibility ...

Quite simply, if the above definition offers some understanding of the meaning of risk, the process of risk assessment is about evaluating the possibility of that outcome, drawing on information that might clarify or inform. We essentially consider a situation, draw from it the information that might help us make an assessment of that situation, and then reach informed conclusions as to the likelihood of the risk occurring. In therapy practice we generally do not undertake a risk assessment per se, as we do not evaluate risk in such general ways. Assessing risk as an idea is too generic and insufficiently focused to be meaningful. Instead, we assess particular aspects of risk, depending on the situation and context. Again, as we considered in Chapter 2, a risk assessment could consider several different possibilities:

- The likelihood of a financial investment gaining or losing money
- How people use buildings and the extent to which they are exposed to harm
- A teacher evaluating the potential hazards of a school trip
- A health and safety inspector reviewing procedures in a laboratory
- A counsellor or psychotherapist considering the likelihood of their client being violent to another person, for example.

In looking at the above scenarios, an *assessment of risk* would be informed by the specific contextual factors of the situation. However, simply focusing on a particular context, such as therapy, still does not provide sufficient detail as to the purpose of the assessment. For example, we might assess for the risk of suicide, or the impact of self-injury, or of safeguarding concerns, or of child protection, or of a terrorist threat, or of violence to others, for example. But we might also assess for the risk of a poor outcome to therapy, or threats to the alliance, etc. The point here is that while it is perhaps okay for us to use the term 'risk assessment' as a shorthand for a range of activities we undertake, when we are actually assessing risk we need to be clear as to the nature and form of the risk we are exploring. There are a number of reasons for this, including:

- Knowing exactly what it is we are looking for to ask the right questions
- To provide clear information on which we can base our evaluation
- To contribute to an audit trail of factors that informed our evaluation
- To ensure we continue to work within the parameters of the therapeutic contract
- To ensure we meet any procedural or policy expectations around specific risk
- To help inform discussions in supervision

- To facilitate the client's full engagement in the process so that they are clear too
- To provide opportunities not only for an assessment of risk, but rather an evaluation of risk to help inform insight, and possibly change.

While all the points above are important, I would draw your attention to the last two. I hope to argue throughout this book that risk assessment should not be an intervention that the therapist *does to* the client, but rather something that is *done with* the client, collaboratively, where possible. Assuming the client has the capacity to engage with the process (which might not always be the case if the client is experiencing mental health distress, for example), they should be encouraged to be an active and equal participant in any dialogue about risk. For myself, and this might seem more about semantics than practice (although I would disagree), I prefer the term risk *exploration* rather than risk *assessment*, as the former implies more a process of collaboration and the latter more a process of procedure. You should obviously use the terms that suit your practice and settings best, but it is something that is worthy of reflection. In this chapter I will offer a general consideration of the issues of a questionnaire or risk assessment tool approach and what I will call a discourse-based approach, and reflect on the relative advantages and disadvantages of each.

Pause for reflection

1 Think about the setting in which you work and consider how the process of risk assessment is 'positioned' (i.e. a task informed by procedure or policy; part of the contracting process; an ongoing dialogue; a collaborative process).
2 What are the therapeutic implications of your answer to the question above?

TICKING BOXES

Over recent years there has been an increase in the use of risk assessment tools and questionnaires to assess risk (Leenaars, 2004). These are typically informed by the plethora of research into specific risk areas, such as suicide and self-injury. If we take suicide for example, there is extensive research that tends to consider the demographic factors that might flag higher risk, such as depression, age, gender, etc. (Appleby et al., 2001; Battle et al., 1993; Hersh, 1985; Reeves, 2010, 2013b; Ruddell and Curwen, 2008). It is difficult to give a clear account of one specific tool or measure that is more relevant than another. Typically, different settings will develop tools for their own purpose, all of which are built around similar parameters. They draw on the research that explores risk factors and include obtaining information around the following domains:

- Gender; age; cultural background; occupation
- Disability and other physical health problems
- Living circumstances
- Relationship status
- Mental health history
- Family history
- Previous suicide attempts, or current suicidal ideation
- Levels of self-care
- Other relevant history, including abuse, adult sexual assault, drug and alcohol use.

This information is then gathered together to form an overall picture of the client and, sometimes, a score is generated based on the information that places the client along a particular continuum of risk. This can be helpful information in that it can flag higher-risk clients. However, it is sometimes hoped that this application of 'science' will provide a high level of predictive value as to the intentions or actions of a particular individual: this is not the actual outcome. Alternatively, some 'risk' questions or statements are included in more generic assessment or benchmarking tools, such as the PHQ-9 (Patient Health Questionnaire; 'Over the last two weeks have you had thoughts that you would be better off dead, or of hurting yourself?'), or CORE-OM (Clinical Outcome in Routine Evaluation, Evans et al., 2002) including six risk statements overall, such as 'Over the last week I have thought of hurting myself', or 'I have made plans to end my life'). The use of risk assessment tools can provide important indicators of *potential* action, but cannot tell us exactly whether someone will act on their thoughts of harm. There is some evidence of the efficacy of the use of such tools in flagging risk factors (Leach et al., 2005).

It could be argued there is a cyclical process here: as research is undertaken into demographic and other social factors that might inform suicide risk assessment, so risk assessment tools and questionnaires are developed around that research. Then, the greater the number of risk assessment tools, the greater likelihood of them influencing the culture of research in the field to drive more research into demographic factors, and so on. Whatever the process here, many counsellors and psychotherapists find themselves in practice situations where they are required to use a risk assessment tool with each client.

There are other important factors here that help to embed the use of such tools into therapy practice, most notably the influence and dominance of the positivist model of research and practice, certainly in the UK but also internationally. This relates to the application of 'science' to the human process in trying to understand and anticipate human behaviour. The epistemological and ontological positioning of much of the research that takes place in the human and social sciences is informed by the same positioning as can be found in the natural sciences, such as chemistry, biology and medicine. Some have argued that, as counselling and psychotherapy has aligned itself more to medicine, the research and practice field has become more dominated by it (Sanders, 2007). That is not to say that medicine and its allied disciplines are a 'bad thing', for that is not the case, but simply that the culture of one has begun to shape the culture of the other with inevitable consequences. As such the 'gold standard' randomised control trial (RCT) continues to be the research evidence of choice, informing not only the delivery of psychological therapies generally but also, and increasingly, the actual practice of the psychological therapies itself (Cooper, 2008; Cooper and Reeves, 2012). In the UK the method of choice in research for practitioner researchers appears to be qualitative, and yet good quality qualitative research continues to fall into the shadow of RCTs. For example, for inclusion in the NICE (National Institute for Health and Care Excellence) Treatment Guidelines for a full range of psychological problems, RCT evidence continues to significantly outweigh other evidence, including qualitative studies. I do not have the space here to enter into a more detailed (and, as such, more qualified) critical appraisal of the influence of positivist approaches against those more informed by a social constructionist model. For these discussions I would recommend Cooper (2008), Roth and Fonagy (2005) and Lambert (2013). It is important, however, to contextualise the growth of the tick-box approach to assessing risk in relation to those models that influence the practice of counselling and psychotherapy.

There are a number of important advantages and disadvantages in using a risk assessment tool with clients: some factors that positively contribute to how we might understand the form and nature of risk as it presents in clients, as well as factors that, if we are not careful, have the potential either to inhibit an exploration of risk or to mislead us about the extent of risk that is present in the client presentation.

Tick boxes: advantages and disadvantages

Risk assessment tools, questionnaires, inventories, etc. have the potential to bring a number of important benefits to practice when working with risk. Some of these are related to the direct work with clients, some to professional and ethical accountability, and others related to the context of therapy.

Direct work with clients: advantages

- *Initial insights*: when clients first register for counselling and are asked to complete a general assessment tool, which will almost certainly contain statements or questions that relate specifically to risk (e.g. Have you thought about ending your own life? Have you hurt yourself during this last week?), they will need to respond to those questions from their own perspective. This might be the first time a client has been asked to think about such things and can provide the potential for an early safe space for the client to reflect on their own experiences.
- *Pacing disclosures*: having reflected on the answers to these questions, the client has time between completing the form and seeing a therapist face to face to talk more. While in some settings this might only be a very short period of time (if the form is completed during the first assessment session), there is still time for the client to reflect on their answers and what they might then say to their therapist. This provides an opportunity for the client to pace their disclosures and only to talk about things when they are ready.
- *Early therapist insight*: how the client has answered these questions about risk (including sometimes whether or not they have omitted them) can provide helpful information for the therapist at the outset of therapy. For example, seeing someone who has scored high on risk questions flags the importance of further exploration, or someone who has scored low on risk questions but high on the others is worthy of note too.
- *Permission giving*: if a risk assessment tool has asked the client about risk, the idea that risk is something to be talked about and explored has already been introduced into the therapeutic process. It is not uncommon for both client and therapist to find this gives permission for a more interpersonal exploration of risk: that it is okay for these things to be talked about.

Direct work with clients: disadvantages

- *Too much, too soon*: while in therapy, the therapist can be mindful as to the level of distress and discomfort the client is experiencing and how they are coping with the early stages of therapy itself. As such, the therapist can be careful about how best to explore issues. Risk assessment forms can sometimes be quite forthright in how questions are asked, and, particularly if care has not been taken over wording, they can propel the client into responding to a number of quite intimate and challenging questions. This can have the potential for arousing further shame and discomfort, and ultimately might silent the client further.

- *Setting agendas*: it is difficult, even for the most experienced therapist, to put aside high scores related to risk. As soon as a therapist is aware of the high risk scores that information has the potential to become important in the process of therapy itself. That is not to say that high risk scores are not important, but risk always needs to be understood in the context of the client's more general social, emotional, psychological, spiritual and demographic context. The danger is that high risk scores can set early agendas for therapy, sometimes overshadowing the more relevant information that might give insight into why risk is present in the first place. That is, the agenda becomes risk management rather than risk exploration.
- *A mechanical experience*: regardless of orientation, becoming a therapist is an extensive and in-depth process that prepares the therapist with the capacity to engage people, often when at their most vulnerable, in a sensitive and empathically informed dialogue around personal material. A client's early experience of therapy can be important in shaping how the alliance might develop. If risk assessment tools are not introduced sensitively and appropriately there is the potential for the client to experience them as mechanistic and thus the therapeutic process itself as devoid of the sort of care they seek.

Professional and ethical accountability: advantages

- *Valuing the contract*: in the early stages of counselling and psychotherapy we typically agree a contract that holds the parameters of therapy safely. We have discussed the nature of the contract previously. It is very common for the contract to refer to how risk will be managed, yet this might still be a source of confusion, uncertainty and anxiety for clients who might wonder exactly what might happen in the event of talking about risk. Risk assessment tools can provide an important opportunity for you and your client to discuss the contract in more detail and anchor such discussions, which might otherwise be abstract, to specific answers the client has given in their assessment forms.
- *Ethical engagement*: ethics can often be abstract ideas that we only ever really pay attention to when faced with a particular dilemma. Whereas in fact ethics inform everything about therapy. The routine use of assessment and risk assessment tools can be used to help us think about the ethics of our work, as we also need to pay attention to how exactly we might respond to the information we receive and how we would use that information to inform and shape our responses to clients.
- *Informing supervision*: the information obtained from risk assessment tools, as with all other verbal and non-verbal information, can be helpfully

taken to supervision for more exploration. While supervision is a space to explore therapy process, among other things, the challenge for us as therapists to address is that we always filter that information through our own perspectives. Client completed information forms bypass that filtering process to an extent and can, therefore, more fully inform supervision discussions.

Professional and ethical accountability: disadvantages

- *Smoke and mirrors – what we see and what we get*: we discussed previously the faith that can be placed in science over the information available through experience. In this instance the danger is that we receive information from risk assessment tools and, because it has been obtained through the use of a risk assessment tool, we either assume it must be correct or don't question its validity any further, or both. That is, we passively receive the information and do not critically reflect on it. The particular danger here is that it is not uncommon for such information about risk to be simply wrong: where high risk is indicated but there is no real risk at all (perhaps because the client misunderstood the form, or believed that by answering the risk questions with high risk they would be prioritised for allocation, for example); or where low risk is indicated but the client is actually at high risk (perhaps because the client misunderstood the form, or felt too embarrassed or shamed to write such information down). We always need to question and critically reflect on the information we receive, even if we believe the source of that information is foolproof.
- *Ethical challenges*: we discussed above the danger of risk assessment information setting the agenda for future exploration, and the same can be true for further action. If we see high risk scores on a risk assessment form, we might automatically assume that we need to act without really thinking about that information any further. We might feel an imperative to act in a way that we consider ethical, but instead act in a way that is potentially unethical because we have lost sight of the needs of the client.
- *Rabbit in the headlights*: we will explore throughout this book how working with risk can raise a number of important anxieties in us as therapists. We can have the potential to feel immobilised by our anxieties and, as such, fail to make any meaningful psychological connection with our clients. In doing this we might prevent ourselves from exploring risk with clients, instead being frozen in the 'headlights' of high risk information on the forms.

The context of therapy: advantages

- *Equitable services and research*: it is important that when clients enter into therapy that they receive a service that is responsive to their needs, but also one that is equitable and fair, and not based on factors that might lead to discrimination. This is the same in risk assessment terms, in that clients need to be given fair and equitable opportunities for their risks to be identified and appropriately responded to. A risk assessment tool that is well researched, with a high level of rigour, can contribute to a more equal identification of risk-based information. Additionally, such information can be used for research purposes, perhaps for the service specifically, for a wider context in which it might sit, such as in health care, and in practice research networks (PRNs), where therapists and organisations work collaboratively to collect data.

- *Demonstration of action and evidence*: a 'paper trail' of evidence can be enormously helpful in demonstrating action in response to risk. As we have discussed elsewhere, practitioner anxiety can be ameliorated by having a clear account both of their actions and the reasons for their actions. Risk assessment tools are generally valued highly in mental health settings and, as such, can contribute a degree of authority and justification for any interventions made around risk.
- *Management of concern*: building on the previous point, if risk is such that further intervention is deemed to be required, information from risk assessment tools can be invaluable in quickly and efficiently communicating concern to other professional groups. While the challenge in practice settings is often to find a mechanism through which effective communication with other professional groups can take place, risk assessment tools can bring a common language to the exchange of concern.

The context of therapy: disadvantages

- *The imperative of science*: it can be very difficult for therapy providers to make decisions about allocation if faced with high risk scores on a validated risk assessment tool. While a therapist's assessment will also be important, when faced with a client who has scored high on risk and a client who has scored low on risk, it can be difficult for services to allocate the 'lower' risk client and make the 'higher-risk' client wait, even if there are concerns about the low risk client. The fear is that if something should happen with the high-risk client (e.g. a suicide), the decision not to allocate would be harder to justify. This was one of the findings from my own research around managing risk in higher education settings (Reeves and Coldridge, 2007).
- *The blunt use of policy and procedure*: many organisations will have in place policies and procedures that inform their therapists how they should respond to risk when identified in therapy. If an organisational expectation is that clients should be referred on for more specialist support if high suicide risk is indicated, then it can be difficult not to do so when a client returns high risk scores, even if the therapist does not believe the client to be at risk (the discrepancy explained above). Organisations can be pressurised into action by virtue of their own policies and procedures in response to risk assessment questionnaire information, regardless of how the client then presents.

- *Shaping the nature of provision*: service development will often be informed by data that is collected through the routine use of such forms. Such information can be invaluable, but there are also dangers of the information not accurately reflecting the nature of the client's presentation. This can be particularly true when thinking about risk due to dynamics such as shame, or an unwillingness to report such issues, or over-reporting.

TALKING ABOUT RISK

Counselling and psychotherapy as 'talking therapies' are inevitably based on discourse: that is, the exchange of dialogue between the client and the therapist that is defined by the nature of the client's concerns, their goals, hopes and preferred outcomes. In turn, the therapist's discourse will be informed by their training, preferred way of working, working context and experience. It is both a simple process of talking but also a highly complex dynamic that has almost unlimited nuances, references and meanings. For many therapists, that is the joy of their work: to work in the subtle, unpredictable and rich field of human relationships and experiences.

With this in mind then, it entirely makes sense for an exploration of risk to be embedded in the discourse of therapy. Why would it be removed from that into a more mechanistic process of ticking boxes and putting crosses on a sliding scale? As we have discussed previously, while risk assessment tools have distinct advantages in the understanding and assessment of risk, they have become more predominant over recent years and, in some settings, are the front-line mechanism for risk assessment. Yet the reality is that whatever information is obtained through the use of such tools, unless that information is to be used unquestioningly and without reference to the client, there inevitably follows a need for a dialogue about the meaning of the information. As such, it could be argued that a discourse-based approach to understanding risk is both inevitable and essential. There are a number of important advantages and disadvantages in talking about risk that we as practitioners must keep in mind.

Talking about risk: advantages and disadvantages

Direct work with clients: advantages

- *Intimacy of exploration*: therapy is a psychologically and emotionally intimate process. In a safe and trusting environment the client might explore areas of their lives they have never talked about before, and be confronted with additional areas and issues they were unaware of. This is certainly true for areas that bring risk, perhaps about living or dying, the safety of others, and self-harm, for example. There is often a relationship between areas of risk and society's unwillingness to talk: risk is often associated with shame and being silenced. A discourse-based approach to exploring risk sits entirely appropriately within this frame and can indeed allow for an exploration, rather than simply two-dimensional assessment, of risk.

- *Flexibility of exploration*: as we have discussed previously, risk is rarely a binary process that equates to being at risk – or not. Rather, risk is a fluid, changing and dynamic process that will reflect any given number of factors at different points. Whereas risk assessment tools are designed to take a snapshot of risk at any given point, it might be argued that a dialogic approach instead engages with a moving image of risk: where those changes and dynamics can be felt and heard in the process of the therapeutic talk.

- *Responsive to client experience*: building on the previous point therefore, dialogic-based approaches to exploring risk can be more responsive to client experience. The therapist is more likely able to change the nuance and intonation of risk exploration in response to the client's experience of both themselves and that process and, as such, risk exploration becomes an important component of the therapeutic process.

Direct work with clients: disadvantages

- *Personal perspectives*: risk is not an area of discussion that is likely to leave us in a neutral place. Whatever the form of risk, such as suicide, self-harm, child protection or violence to others, for example, we are likely to have views and perspectives based on our previous personal and professional experiences. To take suicide more specifically, whether we believe individuals have the 'right' to end their own lives if they decide to, or not, will be powerful influencing factors in how we respond directly with our clients. I, and others, have argued (Adams, 2013; Reeves, 2013b) that it is probably impossible for us to separate our own views out and become 'blank slates' on entering the therapy room, instead we need to be very aware of our own personal responses to risk to help mitigate their impact on the therapy process.

- *Acted out anxiety and fear*: a number of researchers, including myself, have written about the impact of working with risk on the 'self' of the practitioner (Leenaars, 2004). Research has indicated that feelings such as fear, anger, anxiety, impotence, etc. (Fox and Cooper, 1998; Pompili et al., 2002a, 2002b) are often very present when facing risk. As such, we are not always in a position to hear our client's words neutrally, but rather filter them through our own worst-case scenarios, with the potential to respond to clients accordingly.

- *Capacity to tolerate risk*: our capacity to tolerate risk will be influenced by a number of factors, such as our own wellbeing, previous professional experiences, challenges in our own lives, for example. Sometimes we might be able to hear risk and tolerate it, while at other times less so. This will inevitably shape the nature of the dialogue so that it becomes more dependent on our own responses and tolerances, rather than the needs of our clients.

Professional and ethical accountability: advantages

- *More informed decision making*: a dialogic-based exploration of risk has the potential to bring into the frame a full range of information, all of which can further inform how we then subsequently respond to it. As such, the dialogue can help position our clients and us in a collaborative space to discuss and consider risk more fully, and thus help inform outcomes over which clients feel they have some control.
- *Allowing for an interpretation*: ethical expectations of practice direct us to be mindful of the client's needs, autonomy and dignity in a therapeutic process. Risk can sometimes put pressures on those expectations, with therapists balancing the need for safeguarding their client's wellbeing while, at the same time, wanting to respect their autonomy. A dialogic-based approach can allow for those nuances and for professional and ethical actions to be based in a relational approach, rather than an assessment tool approach.
- *Informed positive risk-taking*: ultimately when making decisions *with* clients or, in some rare circumstances, *for* clients, it is essential that we do so with as much available information as possible. Managing risk can sometimes mean we have to go against a client's known wishes, and this demands commensurate care and attention. The nature of the dialogue can be a powerful factor in informing decisions around risk, including positive risk-taking. As discussed in Chapter 10 about positive risk-taking, this has to be a collaborative process in which the client feels fully equal; dialogic approaches to risk exploration can best allow for that to be in place.

Professional and ethical accountability: disadvantages

- *Evidence for decisions*: in the context of a preference for positivism against social constructivism in the delivery of mental health care (and many other contexts too), the danger is that evidence for decisions might be perceived as more reliable if it had been gathered through the application of science (risk assessment tools) rather than discourse. Therapists need to pay particular attention to how their discussions with clients about risk informed professional actions so that they can carefully detail what information was taken into account, and why.

- *Fitting information to justify action*: dialogic approaches to risk exploration can be much more open to interpretation than tick-box approaches. While this can be a strength, as we have discussed, it can also be a disadvantage as it means responses to risk can be more susceptible to interpretation based on what we would want to hear rather than what we actually do hear. If we are risk averse, for example, it can be possible for us to miss references to risk in our clients' narratives.
- *Loss of the client's context*: what risk assessment tools do well is to bring a wide range of contextual information to the table. In working through a series of questions the therapist is presented with a volume of information that helps further inform an understanding of the client's context, as well as their presenting problem. We need to work hard in a dialogic approach to ensure we cover the same ground so that when discussing risk with clients, we do so in a way that is informed by as much information as possible.

The context of therapy: advantages

- *The value of therapist skill*: I have asserted elsewhere (Reeves, 2013b) that, as therapists, we are generally very good at evaluating risk in our clients and that our philosophy of therapy affords us with the best opportunity to respond in a respectful way. We are trained to talk about experience and feelings and, in doing so, can bring our skills and experience into the discourse to facilitate clients to talk about the areas where they feel most vulnerable, including risk. We can often empower clients to name otherwise unspeakable aspects of themselves to help bring about positive change. Our skills in risk exploration are key in effectively working with that risk in practice.
- *Informing and influencing policy*: by being willing to engage in the dialogue about risk, we can then bridge the narrative from the individual therapy context into the wider setting, to inform practice development and how policy and procedure can be most usefully shaped to support practice with risk, rather than undermine it.
- *A contribution to understanding*: beyond the immediate context of therapy, we can use our experience derived from talking about risk to help inform the wider profession. There is generally a dearth of literature that considers working with risk in counselling and psychotherapy. Discourse helps inform research conversations that can, in time, shape practice. The predominance of research into the factor-based approach to working with risk is leading to the increasing use of risk assessment tools, whereas if more research were undertaken into how we might more effectively talk about risk we might be better supported to engage in that narrative.

The context of therapy: disadvantages

- *Interpretation and perspective*: as we have stated previously, the downside of any human exchange is that it is inevitably experienced through particular lenses and perspectives. While that is not a downside per se, in terms of informing practice, policy and research around risk it has the potential to take us down cul-de-sacs and make wrong turns.
- *Hoist by our own petards*: developments in practice are best informed by the collected wisdom of conversations rather than simply a perspective or experience in isolation. When working with risk, a full range of ideas and values needs to be present to help us continue to move to the best practice we can deliver. The danger is that if our experience of risk has been a damaging one, we can look to safeguard our own wellbeing through the development of practice that is both risk averse and back covering. We try to 'tie down' practice in an attempt to avoid the uncertainties and the unknowns. Whereas the uncertainties and unknowns sit at the very heart of our work, including with risk, and have to be at worst tolerated and at best energetically engaged with.
- *Lack of equity and consistency*: through the process of interpretation, fear, anxiety, reactive rather than proactive practice, we run the danger of developing practice that is not consistent and undermines particular groups. For example, clients with severe mental health distress can easily be marginalised through our own fear, which can be exacerbated through a discourse that is rooted more in anxiety than engagement.

TO TALK OR TO TICK BOXES?

Having considered in some depth the relative advantages and disadvantages of risk assessment tools and disclosure-based approaches to risk, we are inevitably left with the question: should we use risk assessment tools, or talk to our clients? While my answer might seem to be more about me positioning myself firmly on the fence, I would say that the integrated use of the two perhaps allows for the best possible outcomes. While my own preference is much more towards supporting myself to talk to my clients about risk and engaging in an exploration of their risky worlds, I also use assessment tools, such as CORE-OM, that flag areas of concern around risk. I find that, in practice, I am able to draw on the advantages of such tools while seeing them as only partly contributing to my overall understanding. They are not the end point in exploring risk, but rather are best used as the starting point. In then talking with my clients I can enter into their world of risk, while using the risk assessment tool information, and further explore meaning, sense, feeling and intent more fully.

WORKING WITH RISK ONLINE

The relative advantages and disadvantages of different approaches to working with risk, as outlined here, apply easily to face-to-face environments but online contact presents many different challenges. While it is still possible to ask clear and direct questions about the nature and extent of risk, some of the information that is available to the face-to-face practitioner, such as non-verbal communication, intonation, silences and micro-responses to questions (eye contact, breathing) are not available in the same way, or at all. Perhaps it is in the face-to-face environment that the integrated use of tools and talk provide for the best opportunity to understand and explore risk.

There is some emerging evidence that young people may prefer online environments when talking about risk, such as risk of suicide (Evans, 2014), as it provides the anonymity and autonomy they prefer. The work of Evans looks specifically at young people's use of online environments to talk about suicidal ideation. Evans asks:

> How can we reconcile our duty of care and to protect with the safety they clearly see as provided by the anonymous online environment? If young people's preference for discussing 'big' problems is via the anonymous environment of cyberspace, is this an indictment of current UK Safeguarding procedures that young people are creatively bypassing by using cyberspace? Another conclusion is that some young people at their most distressed appear to not want a reaction from us or for us to engage in action. Many simply want to be listened to by another willing to go there with them … (2014: 8)

This raises important questions about the nature of contracts for online work, what information is gathered prior to work commencing, how the accuracy of information is verified and the willingness of the online practitioner to still ask important questions about risk and what the individual might want from that contact. But perhaps there is some affirmation in the work of Evans that what people need most from a therapist around risk is the willingness to go to the most difficult places and have the discussions that can bring insight and change.

Chapter summary

In this chapter we have explored the two primary ways in which risk is considered in counselling and psychotherapy: risk assessment tools, and dialogic approaches. We have discussed the current preference for the

(Continued)

(Continued)

application of 'science' in exploring risk and the predominance in the research of a factor-based approach to understanding it, and its implications for us as practitioners. We have considered the relative advantages and disadvantages of these two approaches across three main domains: in direct work with clients; for our professional and ethical practice; and in the contexts of therapy. I have suggested that a combination of these two approaches perhaps brings us the best opportunity to fully explore risk, while at the same time being mindful of the very real disadvantages and dangers that are inherent in both approaches as well.

4

WORKING WITH A RISK OF SUICIDE

Chapter outline

This chapter will consider counselling and psychotherapy with clients who are suicidal. A definition of suicide will be offered and we will reflect on how we might work effectively with the risk of suicide, and to know when we might need to act to help safeguard our client's wellbeing. The chapter will primarily explore how therapists can help clients identify their suicidal thoughts, how suicide can be helpfully talked about in sessions, and how working with suicide potential can be a collaborative rather than a one-way process.

INTRODUCTION

Suicide is a significant public health concern, with the World Health Organization (WHO) estimating that internationally over 800,000 people die each year through suicide, representing one death through suicide every 40 seconds (WHO, 2014). As we will discuss later in the chapter, at the time of writing the number of suicides in the UK is increasing across certain groups and the risk of suicide can be experienced by the professional 'helper' – social worker, psychiatrist, clinical psychologist, counsellor, psychotherapist, mental health nurse and so on – as a significant emotional and professional burden. Research points to the high levels of anxiety experienced in working with suicide potential (Reeves, 2010), and a link has been suggested between ongoing work with suicidal clients and vicarious trauma and burnout (Fox and Cooper, 1998). Counsellors and psychotherapists will often work with clients who present with some suicide potential and need to have the confidence and competence to engage proactively with their clients to establish the level and extent of that risk, and the degree of intent to act on it. This can present many challenges to practitioners who, depending on the context in which they work, may be required to make referrals on to more specialist agencies, if necessary without client consent, for further assessment of risk.

In this chapter I will provide a broad overview of the key considerations when working with clients at risk of suicide, as well as highlighting some key considerations for practice. Additionally, I will explore ways in which we might actively engage our clients in a collaborative process so that they can become active participants in their own wellbeing – taking responsibility for their own safety – as opposed to us as practitioners simply falling into the trap of doing *to* our clients, rather than doing *with*. My discussion here will be around work with adult clients, (i.e. 18 years and over), as I shall discuss the very particular issues of working with suicidal children and young people in Chapter 7 on safeguarding.

DEFINITIONS

De Leo et al. (2006: 12) define suicide as: 'an act with fatal outcome, which the deceased, knowing or expecting a potentially fatal outcome, has initiated and carried out with a purpose of bringing about wanted changes'. While the WHO defines suicide as: 'the act of deliberately killing oneself' (WHO, 2014). As I have noted elsewhere (Reeves, 2013b), defining suicide is not necessarily helpful to counsellors and psychotherapists when working with risk, whereas thinking about what we mean by 'suicidal' is. The former term defines the outcome of an act with intention, while the latter term more outlines a state of being: long-standing, developing or transitional.

In thinking about the term 'suicidal' it is helpful therefore to break this down a little more. At a most general level we can think about suicidal ideation, and suicide intent. Suicidal ideation describes a set of ideas, beliefs and feelings that point towards the possibility of suicide. This may cover quite a wide spectrum, with someone having very fleeting thoughts about suicide in an abstract way, through to someone whose thoughts are more persistent. Suicidal intent is where a person has moved beyond suicidal ideation and their thoughts have become more of an intention to act. Again, there will be degrees of intensity for suicidal intent; with some the intent can be quite strong or immediate, while for others the intention is present, but without any immediacy. Consider the following brief scenarios:

1. Low risk: vague ideation

Rosanna is struggling at work and fearing that she will soon be made redundant. In counselling she has explored coping strategies and says to her counsellor: 'Sometimes, I just wonder whether it is worth it, but I would never do anything.'

2. Low risk: focused ideation

Anton is 76 years old and attending bereavement counselling following the death of his partner. He has good friends and family support, but also feels tired sometimes of the emotional burden of his loss. He says to his counsellor: 'Sometimes I just want to go to sleep and not wake up.'

3. Moderate risk: specific ideation but with some intent

Sally is a 22-year-old drama teacher. She has been depressed for some time and while she has been making progress in counselling, she also feels overwhelmed by her feelings on occasion. She says to her counsellor, 'I sometimes think about taking an overdose.'

4. Moderate to high risk: move to intent

Jake is 19 years old and is socially isolated. He is struggling at university and has little family support. He has been angry and depressed for several months and says to his counsellor, 'I have collected some medication and I am thinking of killing myself.'

5. High risk: specific intent

Zac is 27 years old with a long-standing physical illness that causes him great pain. He has been thinking about how he will cope and says to the counsellor, 'I cannot go on like this. I am going to kill myself.'

Pause for reflection

1   What are your responses to each of the five scenarios above?
2   Do you agree with how they are defined in terms of levels of risk?
3   How might you respond to each client in practice?

If we consider the basic factors that might differentiate risk in the scenarios above. In (1), the client reassures her counsellor that she wouldn't do anything, but talks in a generalised way about how sometimes she questions the validity and struggle of her situation and life. Such questions can be literal but also more existentially reflective and can be important aspects of the therapy process. In (2), while the thoughts are still quite generalised there is a move to something a little more specific. That is, a shift from a very general thought about life, to a more specific statement of not wanting to carry on, albeit expressed passively. In (3), the client is much more specific about her thoughts, with some indication of early intent. She names a potential method (overdose of medication) but with no specific detail about acting on her thoughts. In (4), ideation is much more specific ('I am thinking of killing myself') with reference to acquiring the means to do this (collecting medication). Finally, in (5), the client makes a clear statement of their intention to end their own life. We will consider the particular practice indicators in relation to these scenarios a little later in the chapter.

WHAT DO THE STATISTICS TELL US?

The statistics that relate to deaths through suicide provide some indication of the nature of the problem, while not always portraying a fully accurate picture of it. This is not because the statistics are fundamentally flawed in and of themselves, but because they report on deaths where a verdict of suicide has been recorded, or where there is strong evidence of suicide. There are occasions where death is not recorded as suicide due to a lack of sufficiently strong evidence to support that declaration, but where it is reasonably believed that suicide was the cause. As such, there is the potential for a mismatch between the recorded numbers and the actual numbers.

However, the statistics that are available tell a rather dismal story, with the numbers of suicides in the UK recorded in the thousands. At the time of writing the latest UK Department of Health statistics (DoH, 2014) showed that there was overall an increase in the number of suicides. Figure 4.1 shows the rates of deaths between the genders across age groups, illustrating that males are at three to five times more likely than females to complete suicide right across the age span. This is partly explained in Figure 4.2, which shows the methods selected for suicide. As can be seen, a higher proportion of males selected hanging as opposed to overdose than females. While with many overdoses there is a period of possible intervention with medical treatment that can

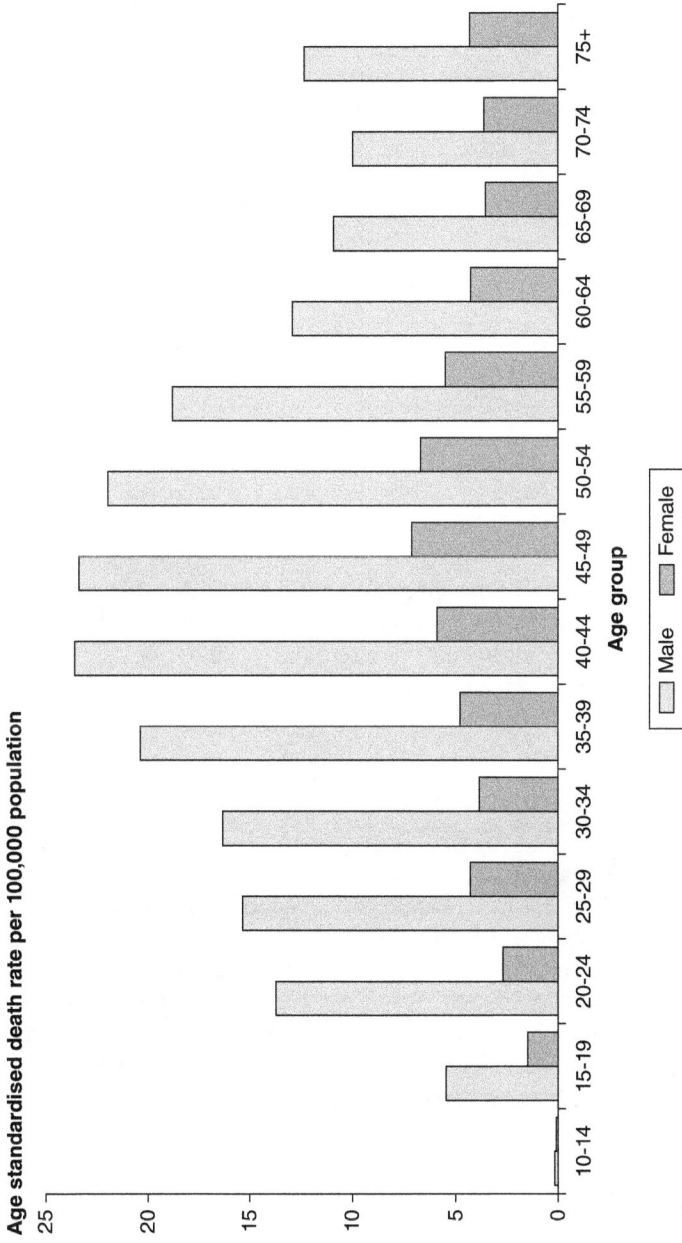

Figure 4.1 *Deaths due to suicide across age and gender*

Source: ONS Reproduced under license: http://www.nationalarchives.gov.uk/doc/open-government-licence/

Males   **Females**

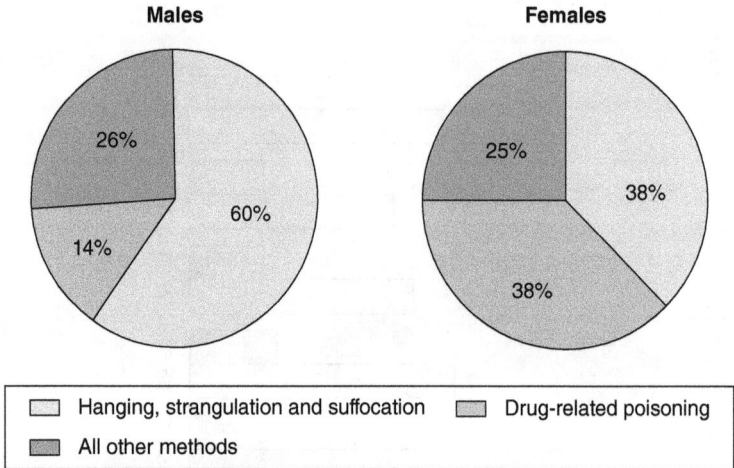

26%   25%
                                              38%
              60%
14%
                              38%

☐ Hanging, strangulation and suffocation   ☐ Drug-related poisoning
☐ All other methods

Figure 4.2   *Causes of death due to suicide by gender*

Source: ONS (ICD10 X60-X84, Y10-Y34) Reproduced under license: http://www.
nationalarchives.gov.uk/doc/open-government-licence/

reverse the effects, with hanging there is very little time for medical
intervention once the act has been completed. This is an important
factor to consider in evaluating the nature and extent of risk: the degree
of lethality of the selected method of suicide.

THE RESEARCH EVIDENCE: RISK AND PROTECTIVE FACTORS

When thinking about suicide risk it is helpful to keep two primary
aspects in mind: risk factors and protective factors. A risk factor for
suicide is something that makes the suicide more likely, while a protective factor is something that makes suicide less likely. A careful
exploration of what the risk factors are, against what the protective
factors are, can be helpful in determining with the client the level of
risk they present with. There are other considerations too, which we
will explore later in the chapter.

Risk factors

Research into suicide predominantly focuses on risk factors – more
specifically, demographic, social and psychological (or pathological)

factors that research indicates make suicide more likely. The research in this area is extensive and indeed risk factors form the primary focus for many studies. Less attention is given to why people might experience suicidal feelings and less still on how we can build both confidence and competence to talk to people about suicide. However, these remain important considerations as risk factors in and of themselves and provide part of the information needed. A list of some risk factors is included in Table 4.1.

Table 4.1   *Risk factors for suicide (Reeves, 2010, 2013b: 33)*

- Gender: males present with greater risk across all age groups
- Age: and particularly males aged between 14 and 49, and over 75
- Relationship status: single; widowed; divorced; and separated
- Social isolation
- Psychopathology, including:

  o Schizophrenia
  o Mood disorders, including depression with hopelessness
  o Psychosis
  o Post-traumatic stress disorder (PTSD)
  o Affective disorders, including bipolar disorder
  o Organic disorders (such as dementia)
  o Personality disorders

- Alcohol and drug use
- Occupation factors: unemployment, retirement
- Occupational groups: vets, medics, farmers
- History of childhood sexual abuse
- Adult sexual assault
- Where there is a specific plan for suicide formulated
- Prior suicide attempts and/or a family history of suicide or suicide attempts
- Physical illness: terminal illness, biochemical or hormonal disorders
- Bereavement or recent trauma
- Recent hospital discharge
- Significant and unexplained mood change
- Self-injury

As can be seen, the list is fairly extensive but difficult to differentiate in practice. It is not uncommon for clients to present with a number of these factors. Indeed, it might be that you can identify with some of them in yourself. Simply presenting with a risk factor does not mean that suicide is likely to happen. The more risk factors a person presents with, the more challenge they may experience in their lives but, again, this does not automatically equate to higher suicide risk. It is important

to be able to talk to clients about their thoughts and feelings in relation
to suicide while, at the same time, using the presence of any risk factors
as important contextual information. For example, a young, depressed
male client who is regularly drinking heavily but with no expressed
suicide ideation might present at some risk in virtue of being male,
young, depressed and drinking, but should the same client talk of
wanting to 'get out of everyone's way', indicating potential suicidal
ideation, the risk becomes more notable due to his demographic and
behavioural characteristics.

Protective factors

While the research into protective factors that might help to prevent
completed suicide is less plentiful than the research into risk factors,
it is sufficient for us to be able to identify some key areas to consider.
When working proactively with risk the presence of any protective
factors is extremely important. The practitioner can help the client
identify those factors for themselves, so they can then be supported
to use those factors in their day-to-day life. The truth is, in working
with suicide risk in therapy it is ultimately the client who will keep
themselves safe, given that therapy is relatively such a short interjec-
tion into someone's life. The task of the therapist in responding to
suicide potential specifically is to help equip the client to be able to
do this, even when faced with crisis. This resilience in the face of
suicidal thoughts is often the difference between life and death.
Table 4.2 outlines some protective factors to consider when working
with risk.

Table 4.2   *Protective factors mitigating the risk of suicide*

- Attending counselling or psychotherapy
- The nature and quality of the therapeutic alliance
- Willingness to talk about thoughts and feelings
- Some capacity for emotional expression
- Informal support networks in community (friends, networks)
- Formal support networks in community (mental health care)
- Family support (and willingness to access it)
- Involvement in interests and activities
- Established successful coping strategies
- Other key individuals the person can access and is willing to talk to
- Options for support 'out of hours', e.g. at night
- Physical activity, such as exercise
- Other important attachments
- A collaboratively agreed crisis plan

Protective factors have often focused on the nature of the *interpersonal* support mechanisms that clients can tap into in between sessions, such as external support agencies, family, friends. However, I would add that the nature of the client's *intrapersonal* self-support mechanisms should be considered as well. In working with suicidal clients I have often noted that it is less about the availability of external support, but rather the client's willingness and ability to make use of the external support, that can determine the extent to which a client is able to look after themselves at times of difficulty. Intrapersonal protective factors might include:

- The client's psychological mindedness
- The client's capacity and willingness to conceptualise and understand their distress
- How or whether the client sees 'self' as a mechanism for support
- The level of ambivalence about wanting to live
- The client's sense of a future
- The client's sense of the potential for change
- The client's level of mental capacity.

This final point is important in that it ties in with legislative considerations around mental capacity, which I will consider now.

LEGAL CONSIDERATIONS

There is insufficient space here to fully detail the legal parameters that inform the nature of work with suicidal clients. I would recommend reading Mitchels and Bond and others (Mitchels and Bond, 2010; Jenkins, 2013; Reeves, 2010) for more in-depth accounts. In this section I will instead mainly focus on the concept of capacity, as outlined in the Mental Capacity Act (2005), and in Scotland the Adults with Incapacity (Scotland) Act (2000). While dealing with issues that are broader than suicide risk, the scope of this legislation is directly relevant for working with suicide risk. Likewise, in more general terms, we need to be assessing a client's capacity at the beginning of therapy to ensure they are making an informed decision about entering into therapy.

The Mental Capacity Act (herein referred to as the Act), assumes that everyone over the age of 18 has capacity to make decisions about their own lives, including receiving treatment (which would include counselling and psychotherapy). Young people between the ages of 16 and 18 are also assumed to possess capacity to refuse treatment, although the

High Court or Court in Session is able to overrule this in certain situations. Importantly, we have the right to make decisions about accepting or refusing treatment, even if that decision might result in our death, and it would be unlawful to assume a person did not have capacity simply because their decision was deemed unwise: we have the right under law to make unwise decisions. In relation to suicide (and given that suicide itself is not a criminal act under UK legislation), the Act allows for an individual to make a decision that might bring about their own death, as long as they have the capacity to do so.

Clearly, in therapy, mental capacity is not the only important consideration and several things need to be balanced together:

- The individual's mental capacity
- The individual's age
- The nature of the contract for counselling, including any limitations to confidentiality
- Any policies or procedures that inform counselling
- The presence of risk factors
- The presence of protective factors (both inter- and intrapersonal).

The law makes allowance for the fact that, at certain times, a professional may make a 'best interests' decision for the client if that action is intended to safeguard the client's immediate wellbeing, such as breaking their confidentiality to access specialist help or crisis intervention. As such, a therapist deciding to break confidentiality following concern of immediate risk of suicide is likely to be protected under law as a 'best interest' decision, as long as the therapist is able to provide a clear rationale for the decision and demonstrate how it was the most effective response to safeguard the client in the circumstances. In thinking about client consent, Bond and Mitchels (2014) offer some useful guidance for therapists to consider:

- For what action is consent being sought?
- Have all the potential benefits, risks and consequences of taking or not taking that action been fully explained and understood?
- Has the person retained the information long enough to properly evaluate it when making the decision?
- Can the person clearly communicate their decision (with help as appropriate) once it is made?
- Is the consent sought for the individual concerned, or is it for the treatment of another person?
- If consent is sought for another person, is that person an adult or a child?
- If consent is sought for a child, does the person giving consent have parental responsibility for the child?

Whatever decisions are made about how to work with suicidal risk, a judgement on the client's capacity to engage with that process is essential. It is not possible for a client who has permanently (e.g. head injury), or temporarily (e.g. psychosis) lost capacity to work collaboratively in keeping themselves safe. See the scenario of Adrian.

Working with capacity: Adrian

Adrian is a 19-year-old male client who is seeing a counsellor in a third sector mental health agency. While he has been using counselling well, the last few sessions have seen his presentation change and his counsellor has been concerned about him. While he still talks quite lucidly, he says that he believes he is possessed by demons and that they require him to demonstrate his immortality. To do this he must walk along the nearby motorway and, regardless of what incidents he might be involved in, he would survive. His counsellor is extremely concerned and shares these concerns with Adrian, who smiles, and then dismisses them, saying that as the counsellor does not hear the voices he could never really understand.

Pause for reflection

1 Do you think issues of mental capacity are relevant here and, if so, are they permanent or temporary?
2 How well do you think Adrian would be able to work collaboratively in keeping himself safe?
3 What information would you need to make a decision about how best to act in response to the high risk he presents himself, and others, with?

THE RESEARCH EVIDENCE: COUNSELLING AND PSYCHOTHERAPY

Counselling and psychotherapy for people who present at risk of suicide can be very effective (Winter et al., 2009). Comtois and Linehan (2006: 167) state that: 'The success of psychotherapy trials for high-risk suicide behavior highlights the importance of psychotherapy's role in the prevention of suicide.' The available research literature generally favours the use of cognitive behavioural therapy (CBT), dialectic behaviour therapy (DBT) and problem-solving therapy (PST). This focus on the more cognitive-behaviourally informed approaches to working with suicide is consistent with the types of methodology used for the studies, primarily RCTs. That is not to say that other approaches, such as humanistic or psychodynamic therapy, are not helpful when working with suicide risk, but that there is less evidence to support their use. This is probably more a statement about the relative value of evidence rather than of the approaches. Winter at al. (2009: 28) state that: 'Both meta-analyses provided a pooled estimate of effect that was indicative of the effectiveness of counselling and psychotherapy in the prevention of suicide.'

Winter et al.'s (2009) review of qualitative studies considered, among other things, the process of therapy with regard to the prevention of suicide. A number of therapeutic factors were identified across a number of studies as being important. These were:

- Respect (Craigen, 2006)
- Understanding (Aoun, 1999)
- Validation of feelings (Cunningham et al., 2004)
- Being non-judgemental (Araminta, 2000).

In summarising the qualitative literature, Winter et al. note the following primary areas of importance:

- *Therapeutic relationship*: the importance of the relationship was identified in responding to suicide risk, and that trust was an essential component of the relationship.
- *Previous experiences*: therapists should take time and care to explore a client's previous experiences of being supported (particularly in relation to self-harm, but arguably in relation to suicide risk also). The client needs to be ready for therapy and premature therapy can do 'more harm than good' (2009: 52).
- *Internal and external worlds*: therapists need to explore how their client experiences their internal and external world, rather than focusing too much on their behaviour. Doing this can leave clients feeling isolated and can create a belief in the client that the therapist in not interested in the whole person.
- *Training*: there is strong evidence of a lack of training for therapists in working with suicidal clients.
- *Knowing when to challenge*: therapists need to demonstrate understanding, respect, validate feelings and be non-judgemental, but also need to know when to challenge clients to address painful issues.
- *Silence*: an overuse of 'therapeutic silence' can hinder the therapeutic alliance with suicidal clients and leave them feeling uncomfortable.

ASSESSING AND EXPLORING SUICIDE RISK

We have explored in previous chapters the subtle differences between assessment and exploration. While the distinction I make is not really a true one, in that assessment can be an exploration, and an exploration can assess, it is helpful to think of these as slightly separate concepts at this stage, in that this allows us to think more fully about the therapeutic tasks in working with suicide risk. In this respect I would suggest that an assessment of suicide risk is about gathering information (risk factors, protective factors and capacity) and making a judgement, preferably in collaboration with your client, about the possible outcome. Exploration is a deeper therapeutic task that provides the client with a space to truly engage with their suicidal thinking so that they can gain further insight and understanding. In doing so, they are better equipped to work to safeguard their wellbeing.

Shneidman (1996: 6), a highly respected suicidologist, writes that:

> our best route to understanding suicide is not through the study of the structure of the brain, nor the study of social statistics, nor the study of mental diseases, but directly through the study of human emotions described ... in the words of the suicidal person. The most important question to a potentially suicidal person is not an inquiry about family history or laboratory tests of blood or spinal fluid, but 'Where do you hurt?' and 'How can I help you?'

This challenge to professionals working with suicide potential in many ways flies in the face of current accepted wisdom – that the truth of suicide potential will indeed be found in the structure of the brain, or in social statistics, or the study of mental diseases, or information about family history, or laboratory tests. Rather, by asking the client 'Where do you hurt and how can I help you?', Shneidman brings to the centre of working with suicide risk a very human exchange.

These seem to be simple questions, but often they are very hard ones to ask. My own research (Reeves et al., 2004) highlighted that experienced counsellors often do not ask clients directly about suicide, even when the client alludes to it. It is difficult to overstate the importance of asking clients about suicide. It is commonly feared that by doing so the danger is that the practitioner will put the thought into the client's mind. There is no research evidence to support this fear; asking about suicide, at worst the level of risk will remain unchanged, but commonly the risk will be reduced, as the client is able to explore their feelings and fears and begin to address them fully.

Consider the dialogue selection below from a therapy session with Elliott.

Talking about suicide: Elliott

Elliott is a 20-year-old male client who has been attending for five sessions of counselling. He has a good relationship with his counsellor, Baz, and no previous suicidal ideation was evident at the assessment. Elliott's depression has continued:

Elliott   There are days when I just feel so … y'know … just so low. It feels like a big, black, heavy blanket smothers me and it is just so hard to breathe. It's horrible.

Baz   Sounds really difficult for you. Like you feel overwhelmed by something that takes your breath away and covers you completely.

Elliott   It does. There are times when … well, y'know …

Baz   Can you say a bit more …

Elliott   It's just that … y'know, days when I feel that it's all too much. That I just wish I wasn't around.

Baz   Wish that you weren't around? What does that mean for you Elliott?

Elliott   Just not here any more. Just not around.

Baz   Elliott, can I ask … when you say 'just not here any more' do you mean that you wish you could go away, or that you sometimes think of ending your life?

Elliott   [Pause] … well, sometimes that I could end my life. Just … I think, what's the point. I can't carry on sometimes and think that would be better.

Baz   So at the worst times you feel that it would be better if you ended your life?

Elliott   Yes.

Baz   Have you thought about what you might do Elliott? Do you feel able to talk about that with me?

Elliott   I knew someone who hanged themselves. I wouldn't want to mess around – y'know, it go wrong and end up in hospital with people pitying. I wouldn't want that.

Baz   So you have thought about hanging yourself?

Elliott   I'm not sure I would actually do it. But that's the thought.

Baz   On a scale of 1–10, 10 being unbearable and 1 being not having feelings at all, how bad does it get?

Elliott   Erm … not sure really … about 7 I suppose.

Baz   So it gets quite bad? And now, as you're talking? How is it talking about this?

Elliott	It's a relief man. Really. I feel so ashamed about my thoughts sometimes and talking ... well, it's a real relief. I suppose at the moment I'm feeling about a 2.
Baz	So talking about it is a relief? Means that you are not quite so on your own with it?
Elliott	Yes. I didn't think this would be okay but you seem to be okay with it so ... well, I am I suppose.
Baz	Okay. So, let's talk about the types of things that make things worse for you – that increase the number, and the types of things that make things better – that lower the number. That okay? It means we can begin to talk together about how you might support yourself, particularly at the bad times.

This transcript illustrates a number of key points that help us think about ways of working with risk, and incorporates aspects of assessment and exploration. To summarise these:

- Elliott is initially tentative about talking about suicide, and alludes to it. His counsellor encourages him to talk.
- When he does talk Elliott introduces a metaphor ('I wish I wasn't around'). This is very common and perhaps speaks of the potential for shame and embarrassment when talking about suicide. However, at this stage the metaphor could mean a number of things, including suicide. The counsellor has a choice: work with the metaphor or ask the 'suicide question'.
- Asking the suicide question is hugely important. Had the counsellor not asked Elliott specifically about suicide there is the potential that it wouldn't have been talked about at all. This would leave Elliott alone with his feelings, and also potentially fearing that it is not okay to talk about them.
- Baz is empathic, understanding, but also very clear when he says 'So at the worst times you feel that it would be better if you ended your life?'
- Baz then continues to explore Elliott's level of intent – how much he thinks in detail about his death and whether there is any evidence of planning. This results in Elliott talking about hanging and that he wouldn't want to 'mess around'. This statement does not clarify *whether* Elliott intends to act on his thoughts, but does indicate a considered level of lethality around a selected method, which increases the risk of Elliott's death should he carry out his thoughts. It is important for Baz to follow this up and clarify.
- Baz repeats Elliott's words, which can be effective in enabling the client to reflect on their narrative by hearing it repeated. In response to this Elliott clarifies intent, to an extent, by saying that he's not 'sure [he]

would actually do it. But that's the thought.' This statement shows Elliott taking a step back from the immediacy of thought, but the risk is still very present.

- Bill asks Elliott to consider his level of distress on a 10-point scale. There are different ways of doing this, such as asking Elliott to describe the intensity of his thoughts in words. However, it can be a simple and effective way of facilitating the client to consider the nature and extent of their risk and can be used in an ongoing way in a 'keep safe' plan, or crisis plan (see the next section).
- Elliott talks about his worst feelings (7), and his current feelings (2), and Baz could also ask Elliott to rate his best feelings. This provides a sense of the scale of the distress for Elliott, and again equips them both to think about self-care strategies later.
- Baz checks out with Elliott whether he feels okay in talking about suicide. This provides an opportunity for: (a) a chance to check out the wellbeing of the client; (b) an affirmation of the client's feelings and perspective; (c) a contribution to a collaborative position; (d) affirmation of the therapeutic alliance; (e) a frame in which to continue the discourse; (f) a chance for the therapist and client to consider the client's level of resilience in the face of their suicidality.
- Baz then moves on to help Elliott think about the risk factors that influence him particularly, and the protective factors that might then be used to inform a crisis plan.

Ultimately, Baz and Elliott need to reflect on their contract for counselling and, assuming Elliott has the capacity to do so (which appears to be the case given how responsive he is to Baz's questions, with no evidence of any cognitive impairment), think about whether Elliott needs additional support to help in managing, or whether counselling continues to be a safe, contained and respectful space.

HELPING CLIENTS TO KEEP SAFE

If you have genuine reason to believe that your client is at immediate risk then it is important to talk to them about how additional support might be put in place. If your client is unwilling or unable to consent to you seeking out additional support then, preferably following consultation, it is important that you act, if necessary without your client's consent. Albeit this would be a final option, having exhausted any other means of gaining consent. The questions highlighted earlier regarding consent are useful here.

Assuming you decide against referral on to other services, you need to think about how you work proactively with the risk as presented. This has to be a collaborative process as, when the client leaves your room, their level of safety and capacity to self-care at a point of crisis will be beyond your scope for further assessment and intervention. Ultimately it is impossible to accurately predict the behaviour and actions of another, rather you should use information to support best practice decisions based on risk, protection and capacity. One way of achieving this is to negotiate a crisis plan, or 'keep safe' plan, that your client can take away from the session and use as a resource.

Such plans are different from 'no harm' contracts (where the client makes a promise or commitment to the therapist not to harm themselves between sessions). Such contracts are generally unsupported by the evidence base and some have asserted that such plans are usually employed as a means of avoiding a more thorough assessment of risk and have the potential to be emotionally coercive; as such, they have the potential to meet the therapist's needs rather than those of the client (Beulow and Range, 2001; Miller et al., 1998). A crisis plan, on the other hand, actively supports the client in taking responsibility for their own wellbeing.

Elements of a crisis plan

Depending on the age and capacity of the client to understand the information, the therapist needs to make a judgement about how best to develop such a plan. Usually it will be possible to talk with the client about the different aspects and record them in a way that the client can later access, such as in writing or in audio form, for example. You need to talk to your client carefully about risks, helpful factors and strategies they can use. As such, a typical crisis plan might contain the following elements:

- The actual risk being considered (e.g. thoughts of taking an overdose)
- The times when the risks are likely to be at their highest (e.g. at night)
- 'Red flags' the client might be aware of that could trigger such thoughts (e.g. when they are alone)
- Factors that make the feelings worse, being as specific as possible (e.g. alcohol or drugs)
- Factors that make the feelings better, being as specific as possible (e.g. being around people)
- Who is available to offer informal support (e.g. family, friends)

- Who is available to offer formal support (e.g. a crisis team, Accident and Emergency, a telephone helpline), and ensuring details such as telephone numbers are recorded on the plan
- What might make accessing support less likely (e.g. not wanting to wake someone up)
- What might make accessing support more likely (e.g. agreeing contact with someone in advance)
- Intrapersonal mechanisms for self-care (e.g. meditation, breathing techniques, distraction, etc.)
- A date for review (which will usually be the next session).

The client needs to be reassured that such plans can take a few sessions to develop into something that is most useful, and that part of the plan is to review what worked and what didn't work on a regular basis. The client owns the plan and it belongs to them; they need to feel that they are able to use it as a supportive tool in their lives. The therapist can make a copy of the plan for their own records, which additionally demonstrates the therapist having fully engaged with risk and working proactively and ethically.

KEY POINTERS FOR GOOD PRACTICE

In bringing these considerations together there are a number of key indicators for good practice in counselling and psychotherapy with clients who present a suicide risk. These points help support good practice (Reeves, 2013b: 12):

- Ensure you take time and care over contracting and never assume a client's understanding without carefully checking it out.
- Don't rely on 'stock' phrases in contracting (e.g. 'risk to self and others') that might be very familiar to us but less so to a distressed and vulnerable client attending therapy for the first time – explain what you mean in accessible language.
- Be clear as to any factors that might inform or shape the nature of agreements you might make with clients about therapy (e.g. your working practices in response to suicide).
- Be aware of what services and options exist in your area for onward referral, if necessary. Knowledge of these can help inform risk management planning as well as onward referral in crisis. Know of these services before you need them and, if possible, make some form of contact with them to talk about referral procedures (and how, as a private practitioner, you might expedite a referral quickly if needed).

- Take time and opportunity to carefully reflect on your own feelings and responses to suicide, and how you have reached this position.
- Think about how you might talk to clients about their suicidal thinking and perhaps practise in supervision.
- Be willing and open to asking all clients about the potential for suicide, when appropriate.
- Be aware of the apparently very good reasons we might come up with for not having talked with a client about suicide (e.g. they were too upset to ask) and reflect on the fact that there are, in fact, very few good reasons why we might not ask about suicide.
- Asking about suicide will not put the thought into the client's mind – instead it will more likely reduce risk.
- If a client is vulnerable, think about collaboratively developing a crisis plan with them: an 'action plan' that is rooted around interpersonal support options (helplines, crisis teams, access to a GP) and also intrapersonal support options (things the client can do for themselves as self-support, such as meditation, exercise, distraction or focusing techniques) that they can take away, and that outlines risk triggers and lists what actions and support the client might access as a means of supporting themselves (detailing those supports, such as telephone numbers).
- Making decisions about how to respond to suicide potential should never be informed by 'gut feeling', instinct or any other potentially magical process. Instead, use your knowledge, training, what the client says, what the client doesn't say, how they present, discussions in supervision (if time allows) and so on, to develop an informed and explicit rationale for actions that you can clearly articulate to yourself, your supervisor and, most importantly, your client.
- Ensure you record appropriately any concerns regarding risk, how you responded and what the outcome was (including your client's part in that process).
- Ensure you take the time and opportunity to reflect on the ethical aspects of how you work and that you read relevant guidance on legislation that might be pertinent in your work with suicidal potential.

Chapter summary

In this chapter we have considered what is meant by suicide, as well as considering the concept of suicidality in more detail. We have differentiated between *suicidal ideation* and *suicidal intent*, and looked at how these concepts are relevant for practitioners to consider explicitly with their clients. We have considered how research has informed our understanding of suicide, particularly around the development of risk factors. However, we have also considered the importance of protective factors and making an evaluation

(Continued)

(Continued)

of the client's capacity to work in counselling when they are suicidal. We have demonstrated ways in which therapists can ask questions about suicide, as well as then developing further dialogue to help the client reflect on the nature and extent of their thoughts. In considering a dialogue between Elliott and Baz we have also explored in some detail aspects of the dialogue that can be helpful. We have outlined key areas to consider in developing crisis plans, or 'keep safe' plans in working with suicide risk proactively, as well as finally outlining some key good practice indicators.

5

WORKING WITH SELF-INJURY AND SELF-HARM

Chapter outline

A working definition will be offered and a differentiation made between 'self-injury' and 'self-harm'. It is important to view these separately (as well as seeing the links between the two), as this allows practitioners to be more inclusive in their thinking of harm. Types of harm will be outlined, as will their purpose and intention. Self-injury and self-harm will be described as coping strategies (although this will be developed in the chapter), but the relationship between harm and suicide potential will be explored. How practitioners might work with clients collaboratively in this process will be highlighted.

INTRODUCTION

The generic term 'self-harm' is an interesting one because it is often used interchangeably to describe several different types of behaviours that each present the therapist with slightly different challenges in working with risk. In fact, some readers might wonder why I have included a chapter on self-harm at all, given that it is usually constructed within an idea of coping, living, surviving and managing. In that context, self-harm is sometimes viewed as less a risk but rather a process of survival. However, there are a number of aspects I would like to unpack here and will explore these points throughout this chapter.

I will focus less on the therapeutic meaning and ways of working therapeutically with self-harm as more detailed accounts can be found elsewhere (Gardner, 2001; Turp, 2002; Reeves, 2013a). This chapter is more about how self-harm might present as a risk in counselling and psychotherapy and the particular considerations to be taken into account when working with, and responding to that risk.

But back to the unpacking: I will begin the chapter by considering what we mean by the definitions that underpin 'self-harm' and then present two scenarios that might help demonstrate why thinking about self-harm as a risk can be a useful position for therapists to take. We will then explore, in the light of the definitions I have offered, the therapeutic implications of those definitions in relation to risk and how therapists might work with their clients in this context.

Before I begin, however, I would like to make an important philo-sophical point that underpins my writing on self-harm and that also has relevance for how we think about it as a presentation of risk. Much is written about self-harm (although taken as a whole, less so specifi-cally for counsellors and psychotherapists), and much of that writing takes a position that differentiates between those who self-harm, and those who don't. They offer an idea of a clear difference between a group of people who engage in behaviours that are ultimately harmful as a means of coping with feelings, and then the rest of us who are well, presumably, pretty well adjusted and able to freely express our difficult feelings all of the time. This is a view I would like to challenge and not one I subscribe to in my writing, my practice nor indeed in my life as a whole.

It is my assertion that there are times when we all self-harm: as a consequence of difficult or challenging feelings we do things or act in certain ways that have the result of being harmful. Such behaviours clearly exist on a continuum, which I will explore further in the section on definitions, but it is a process that we can all relate to. For example, I might come home from a busy day at work and have a few glasses of wine because I wish to be social with friends. However, I might come home from work and have too many glasses of wine because I am angry about something that has happened, or feel stressed or overwhelmed, and 'just need to relax' – even though I might wake up with a hangover and feel unwell, facing another day at work; then the wine became a mechanism of expression rather than social interaction. Clearly I am not suggesting that too many glasses of wine after a stressful day at work is the same as cutting open an arm in response to overwhelming feelings of pain and self-disgust. However, taking away the detail and severity of the behaviour, the *process* is not too different. That is, the enactment into a behaviour or action that has the potential to cause harm as a consequence of difficult and unexpressed feelings.

What is the point of my assertion? Why make an issue about how a 'them and us' approach to self-harm is not helpful? There are several reasons: a 'them and us' position pathologises 'them' and leaves 'us' untouched; separating ourselves out from such a process makes it harder for us to connect in therapy; the insights available to us through exploring our own self-harming behaviour can be profoundly important in connecting with the client's frame of reference; and thinking about our own process can help support us in working with the aspects of risk that emerge from our clients. Quite simply, it is a shared human experience that is best differentiated at the level of the actual behaviour, rather than the underlying process. I am sure this is a contentious position for some, and I would encourage reflection on this.

Pause for reflection

1 Do you agree with the assertion that we all self-harm in some ways, albeit along a continuum of behaviour and severity?
2 If so, can you identify ways in which you self-harm and whether there are common situations that might trigger this (e.g. particular feelings you find difficult to express)?
3 What are the implications for this in working with self-harm in therapy, and in recognising the risks that might be present?

DEFINITIONS

There are several definitions of self-harm that help inform our understanding. NICE (2011: 3) states that self-harm is:

> any act of self-poisoning or self-injury carried out by an individual irrespective of motivation. This commonly involves self-poisoning with medication or self-injury by cutting. There are several important exclusions that this term is not intended to cover. These include harm to the self arising from excessive consumption of alcohol or recreational drugs, or from starvation arising from anorexia nervosa, or accidental harm to oneself.

This is an interesting definition of self-harm as it contradicts other writing in the field. It talks about an action '*irrespective of motivation*' that could, presumably, include suicidal intent. Whereas, for many (and I would include myself here), the motivation of self-harm is an important differentiating factor from suicidal intent: the former is often about coping and the latter about wanting to die. This explains some of the confusion in the research, which often talks about suicide and self-harm as being on the same continuum. There is a statistical conundrum to reflect on here. The assertion is that self-harm is, in itself, an indicator of higher suicide risk in virtue of the fact that many people who die through suicide have a history of self-harm. The 'other side of that coin' is that the majority of people who self-harm do not go on to end their life through suicide. So while self-harm can be an indicator of higher suicide risk, taken into account with other risk factors it is not the precursor to suicide that many have suggested.

The NICE definition specifically excludes alcohol and drug use and eating disorders from their definition of self-harm. The Royal College of Psychiatrists (2010: 21) also includes suicidal intent in their definition when they say self-harm is an action, 'irrespective of the type of motivation or degree of suicidal intent'. Babiker and Arnold (1997: 2), for example, write that self-harm, 'is an act which involves deliberately inflicting pain and/or injury to one's body, but without suicidal intent'. I have offered a summary of the key points in the definitions previously (Reeves, 2013a: 5), which I reproduce here. Self-harm can:

- Be directed against the body (for example, cutting, burning), which might be termed as self-injury
- Include behaviours without immediate impact, such as eating disorders, risky sexual behaviour
- Be planned and form part of an habitual pattern, or may be unplanned and spontaneous
- Be about coping, living, surviving and self-worth
- Have a relationship with suicide potential, particularly in the context of other risk factors.

We can see how the research field can be confusing and misleading, with different definitions and constructions of the same thing. It is impossible to say which is right and which is wrong, but rather better to be clear here as to the terms I am using in this discussion. I would suggest that, for counsellors and psychotherapists, it is very helpful indeed to use the terms 'self-injury' and 'self-harm' to describe slightly different groups of behaviours, and particularly so in relation to working with risk. In referring to self-injury and self-harm I am excluding suicidal intent, but will consider when risk of death begins to emerge as part of the self-harming process. Babiker and Arnold (1997: 4) offer a number of different categories of behaviour:

Self-injury/mutilation

- Cutting
- Scraping
- Burning
- Banging
- Hair pulling (trichotillomania).

Other marginal self-injurious behaviours

- Smoking
- Danger sports
- Reckless driving
- Workaholism
- Over-exercise.

Self-destructive behaviours

- Eating disorders
- Substance abuse
- Sexual risk-taking.

Self-harm

- Suicide
- Parasuicide
- Overdose.

Factitious disorders

- Munchausen's disorder
- Simulated illness.

Somatising disorders

- Skin disorders
- Pain
- Accident proneness.

Body enhancement

- Cosmetic surgery
- Tattooing

- Piercing
- Bleaching.

There are aspects of Babiker and Arnold's categorisation here that we might debate, but for the sake of brevity and usefulness in actual practice I would offer the following breakdown of behaviours:

- *Self-injury*, to include behaviours with direct and immediate consequence, such as cutting, burning, banging, ingesting dangerous substances (including of medication), for example.
- *Self-harm*, to include behaviours with indirect and deferred consequence, such as over-exercise, eating disorders, smoking, alcohol and drug use, sexual risk-taking, for example.

There are, of course, some behaviours with the potential to sit in both groups, such as alcohol and drug use that, when taken to excess, or in combination, can lead to an immediate consequence. However, in more general terms the distinction I offer here centres on the impact of the behaviour: whether it has *immediate and direct* consequence, or an *indirect and deferred* consequence. In the light of this definition we might be able to make more sense of my earlier assertion that we all self-harm (how many of us over-work, or over-exercise, for example), although we might not all self-injure. We can then place each behaviour on a continuum of severity, although the scope of that continuum is typically much narrower when referring to self-injury than it is to self-harm. For example, if someone cuts themselves, then the injury is real and present, direct and immediate, although the severity and degree of cutting can clearly vary. If someone over-works, the deferred nature of the impact can vary considerably over time, and from person to person. These are important considerations when working with risk.

WORKING WITH RISK, SELF-INJURY AND SELF-HARM IN CONTEXT

The context in which counselling and psychotherapy takes place when working with self-injury and self-harm is important here when reflecting on risk. As we discussed in earlier chapters, while as individuals we can be risk tolerant or risk averse, so can institutions and organisations. It may be possible to draw some general conclusions about the different types of organisations, such as that statutory settings (health and social care) are more likely to be risk averse than practitioners working independently, when they can frame their own parameters around risk, however these sorts of conclusions are ultimately limited and can often be wrong. I am aware of services located in the statutory sector that work very proactively with risk, perhaps because they have the structure, procedures and referral routes already established to enable them to do so, while some third sector organisations or independent practitioners might be highly risk averse. I know of several counselling organisations that insist clients stop self-injuring prior to agreeing to therapy. While this might appear to be contradictory both to the ethos of counselling and psychotherapy, and the shared understanding of the process of self-injury, it does perhaps speak of the setting's capacity to tolerate risk.

It is important for each practitioner to be very aware of the implications for their practice of the setting in which they work, and to know and understand any policy or procedural expectations that might shape their therapeutic interventions. Making decisions with clients about how best to respond to risk when it emerges in the therapeutic process will always be contextualised by the setting in which therapy is taking place and how that setting has informed the nature of the contract. Ultimately, working appropriately with risk is a combination of a number of factors, that include the extent and nature of risk as it presents; the clients' capacity to keep themselves safe and to have psychological insight into the risk process; the therapist's capacity to tolerate risk and their capacity to have insights into the risk process; and the context of therapy and what that might demand in relation to specific action, (e.g. the management of confidentiality and referral options).

THE RISK IN SELF-INJURY

While the shared understanding of self-injury is that it is about coping and surviving, this is not always the case and it is important that practitioners remain mindful of the possibility of risk in the process. Risk might helpfully be understood in terms of a continuum, ranging from injury with low likelihood of significant harm, such as minor cuts and small burns, through to where the self-injuring process has the potential to bring about the death of the client, even if that is not their intention. Clearly, in making such a differentiation here I am not implying that one is more important than the other. In terms of working therapeutically, it is important to pay attention to and actively engage with all types of self-injury in the process. In relation to risk, however, they may require different types of interactions with the client. Consider the scenario with Beth.

Risk and self-injury: Beth (1)

Beth has been seeing her counsellor, Alice, for several weeks. At assessment Beth talked about how she has cut herself for some years following family estrangement and physical abuse perpetrated by her mother. She did not particularly want to discuss her self-injury in the sessions, saying it was 'part of her' and more the symptom of problems, rather than the problem itself. As far as Beth was concerned she managed her self-injury well; rather, she wanted to look at the historical issues she felt were more pertinent.

This is not an uncommon presentation in therapy, with the client understanding their self-injury, particularly in the context of the issues that have led to it. Beth conceptualises her self-injury as a coping strategy that 'belongs' to her and one that she feels she manages effectively. At this stage the task is for the therapist to ensure that Beth knows she can revisit a discussion around her self-injury at any stage and to specifically check that Beth feels in control of the process and that, in her view, it does not constitute any risk.

Risk and self-injury: Beth (2)

As the counselling progresses Beth talks about some quite distressing material. She reports to Alice that her self-injury has got worse and sometimes she feels really bad. She is still reluctant to talk about her self-injury and tells Alice that she has read online that sometimes self-injury can get a little worse as the person begins to explore the issues that are causing the distress.

There are a number of aspects here that Alice needs to be mindful of:

- Beth is sufficiently concerned to have raised this with Alice
- Beth says her self-injury has 'got worse' – although it is not clear what that means
- Beth says she feels 'really bad' – although it is not clear what that means
- Beth remains reluctant to talk about her self-injury, even though she has raised it in the session
- Beth is accessing online information about self-harm
- Beth believes that her self-injury might become worse as part of the therapy process.

In responding to the changing nature of risk, Alice needs to have the confidence to talk about these issues to Beth. She still needs to be respectful of Beth's right not to talk about things, but that should not deter from asking questions. Key questions for Alice might be:

- When you say the self-injury has got worse Beth, can you tell me in what ways? For example, are you cutting yourself more frequently or more severely?
- If you are cutting yourself more severely Beth, do you still feel able to look after it yourself? Do we need to think about whether you might need some medical help? Could you perhaps tell me the places you are cutting as some are more vulnerable to cuts than others?
- You say you feel 'really bad' Beth and I suppose I am not sure what that means. Do you mean that the feelings you usually have are getting worse, or are you saying you have thoughts about ending your life?
- It sounds like the online information is helpful to you Beth. Can you tell me a little more about what information you are accessing, as some of it is not always accurate or helpful? I could give you some information about useful sites you might be able to visit if you are interested.
- Sometimes self-injury does become worse when we start therapy, but not always. Would it be useful if we spent some time talking about how you might look after yourself as you talk about these difficult things?

My intention here is not to provide a blueprint or script of what you should say in such situations, but rather to illustrate the importance of being willing to talk openly and directly about issues, even if the client is reluctant to do so. You are still able to follow your client's lead with this, but asking the direct questions is important and might facilitate further discussion.

Risk and self-injury: Beth (3)

Beth arrives at a session quite distressed. She says that she feels her self-injury has gone 'out of control'. She says that she is cutting most days and sometimes a couple of times per day, and that the cuts are deeper. She is frightened about going to hospital for treatment as she is fearful of what they might say, but some cuts have not stopped bleeding and she doesn't know what to do. She fears that some might also have become infected and has been feeling quite unwell: feverish, disturbed sleep, no appetite and occasionally vomiting.

This situation has now moved into a high-risk scenario: both from regarding Beth's emotional wellbeing but also her physical health.

Additionally, the self-injury has changed from being in control and managed, to out of control and unmanageable. It is important that Alice responds sensitively, empathically but also directly, naming her concerns *and* the action that needs to take place. Alice said to Beth:

> Beth, I hear how frightened you are and that you don't know what to do. I want to help and support you with this and to continue to offer you counselling, but the first priority is to ensure you are safe. I am worried about your health because of the cuts that won't stop bleeding, and also the possible infection and how that is making you feel too. We need to arrange for you to go to Accident and Emergency and receive the help you need as you are very vulnerable currently and are at risk. I hope you will give me permission to set that support up for you?

There is a challenge here for Alice: to work with respect for the trust and the strength of the therapeutic alliance, but also to respond to the very real risks Beth is presenting with. Alice carefully and calmly outlines the risks very specifically, while also doing so from an empathic, and not critical or panicked, position. It is important, wherever possible and practicable, to obtain client consent prior to taking any action, to ensure that the process remains collaborative, respectful, and that Beth feels able to return to therapy. However, should Beth refuse consent in the above scenario, and if she cannot be persuaded, it is my view that Alice should act in Beth's best interests and contact her GP, or call for an ambulance. The attempts at obtaining consent do not end if the client initially refuses, but continue throughout the action, wherever possible and appropriate. Not acting would leave Beth alone, potentially isolated, frightened, as well as continuing to bleed from cuts that are not healing and at risk of infection and possible septicaemia. While such actions are not easy steps to take, the wellbeing of the client is paramount and we should have the confidence to act if the information available to us indicates immediate risk.

THE RISK IN SELF-HARM

The scenario with Beth, above, illustrates a change in the nature of risk as her self-injury became more chaotic and dangerous. The nature of risk in self-harm can be as immediate, but is often harder to judge and can present slowly over time, taking both the client and therapist by surprise. Self-harm, such as eating disorders, can be particularly diffi-cult to work with as clients can easily mask the very negative effects of the behaviour, through wearing clothes that hide the weight loss, for example, yet eating disorders, particularly anorexia nervosa, can prove fatal if not responded to.

Other forms of self-harm might lead to risk, but not as a direct consequence of the client's behaviour. This is a key aspect that differ-entiates self-harm from self-injury (discussed previously), in terms of the indirect and deferred nature of the harm caused. Consider the scenario of Matt.

Risk and self-harm: Matt (1)

Matt is a young male client who has been referred to counselling to see Kathy, a counsellor, by his academic tutor at university. Matt is quite depressed and, following assessment, also experiences very low self-esteem and poor body image. This latter point is particu-larly difficult for Matt, as he feels unable to dress or undress in front of friends, cannot consider the possibility of a relationship, wears clothes to mask his *'disgusting, weak body'* and avoids social interac-tions and physical contact with others. While Matt is very isolated and low in mood he does report things he tries to do to help. He goes to the gym four times per week as he is trying to build muscle mass and improve his body image, as he feels doing so will *'solve a lot of problems'.*

Matt's presentation is again not uncommon, related to gender and age. The incidence of body image problems among young males is noted in the literature (Walker and Murray, 2014), perhaps as a result of an increase in the availability of men's health and fitness magazines and the perpetuation of the 'six pack' culture and perfect male body shape. Kathy notes the importance of helping Matt with his low self-confidence and issues around body image. She also notes the positive step Matt is taking in trying to look after himself by attending the gym, but also realises that such actions, while appearing to be of benefit, also speak of Matt not improving his body image, but rather improving his body: the changes are external rather than changes in perceptions of self. At this stage Kathy does not feel there is any risk (Matt does not have any suicidal thoughts), and has not conceptualised Matt's use of the gym as potential for self-harm.

Risk and self-harm: Matt (2)

The outcomes measure Kathy is using is indicating some improvement in Matt's depression. She talks this through with Matt who
agrees, saying that he feels he has some more energy. He doesn't feel
quite so low and this is helping because it enables him to go to the
gym more regularly, now every day. He doesn't feel that he is making
the gains he would like at the gym and has done some research on
the internet to see how he might help himself more.

Kathy is pleased about the improvement in Matt's level of depression and
thinks that he is using the counselling well. It is always important to keep
in mind the relationship between depression and other factors. For
example, in suicide risk an improvement in depression can sometimes
increase suicide risk as the person has more energy to act on their
thoughts, depression (in some instances) being an inhibiting factor.
Likewise, in the case of Matt his improved depression has not changed his
poor self-esteem and body image, and he now has the energy to act on
these concerns. There is a risk here related to Matt's increased use of the
gym *in the context of* him wanting to change his body shape. The self-
harm process can be very insidious and not always apparent. It would be
helpful for Kathy to explore this with Matt by asking him something like:

> On one hand it sounds very positive that you are going to the gym to look
> after yourself Matt, but I also wonder how much this is to do with how
> you feel about your body and whether this might also be making you
> worry more and then perhaps push yourself too much? I wonder what
> your thoughts are about that?

While Matt might not recognise Kathy's concerns, it does put the
possibility on the therapeutic agenda for Matt to reflect on.

Risk and self-harm: Matt (3)

Matt comes into counselling with cuts and bruises to his face. He says
that he got into a fight while out a few days ago. He also says that he
has been feeling very irritable and unsettled. He is pleased that he
has been making some progress at the gym, but puts this down to
the steroids he has been taking for a few weeks. He hadn't mentioned
this earlier as he wasn't sure what Kathy might have said, as he knows

they can be harmful. However, he feels it is a risk work taking and, while he is taking them, he might as well push himself as hard as he can: he now attends the gym 2–3 times per day and although he feels physically and emotionally exhausted, he hopes it will work out.

While there are occasions when risk related to self-harm presents as life-and-death scenarios, more commonly they relate to slow deterioration and increasing concern. However, the same principles apply to the work with Matt as with Beth, in that the role of the counsellor here is to empathically challenge Matt's behaviour and bring the nature of the risk into the counselling room. The risks, as they present here, include:

- The improvement in Matt's depressive symptoms but not change in his low self-esteem and body image
- His increasing use of the gym to very high levels
- His use of steroids and the effects these can have on levels of mood, aggression and impulsivity
- Increased anger and irritability
- Getting into fights with others
- Self-reported physical and emotional exhaustion
- A determination to keep 'pushing' himself while at the same time acknowledging the problems.

While Kathy might not feel that a point has been reached where she might break Matt's confidentiality, there is a good rationale for exploring with Matt the increasing levels of risk and how his situation might continue to deteriorate over time. She might provide him with information about the dangers of steroid use and suggest additional support to help him with this. She might speak with Matt about involving his GP, so that he can be helped medically but also receive information about self-care. If the concerns are clearly expressed, it might be that Matt agrees to speak with his GP and receive additional help, particularly if, deep down, he is concerned about the negative changes in him as a consequence of his steroid use. If Matt refuses it is likely that, at this stage, Kathy would respect his wishes for her to maintain confidentiality, for fear of rupturing the therapeutic alliance. However, indicators for acting without Matt's connect might include:

- Increasing use of steroids with noticeable and detrimental effects on Matt's physical and emotional wellbeing
- Evidence of early onset psychosis, that might be triggered as a drug-induced reaction or as a consequence of exhaustion

- Increasing episodes of violence to others or an increase in other risk-taking behaviour that might cause immediate harm
- Evidence of a lack of mental capacity, brought about by his steroid use, excessive exercise and emotional distress.

The factors outlined above are hard to measure in any certain way. As with any risk, we need to make our best judgements on each situation based on the presenting information available, both generic factors that relate to risk and specific factors that relate to the client's presentation. If we are concerned about a client's immediate wellbeing then we need to act to help safeguard their welfare, with their consent if at all possible.

The relationship between self-injury, self-harm and suicide potential

Based on the scenarios with Beth and Matt it is useful briefly to visit the relationship between self-injury, self-harm and suicide potential. I use the phrase 'suicide potential' here, as opposed to suicidal intent, as the client might not intend to end their own life but their actions might put their lives at risk. This is why it is important for us to think beyond the accepted understanding of self-injury and self-harm as mechanisms of coping, and include in our thinking the possibility that, without an intention, a coping strategy might become life-threatening, as in the case of Beth. If the intention is to die, then we must consider ways of responding to suicidal intent. If the intention is to live, but the actions become life-threatening, we must consider suicide potential and act accordingly.

GOOD PRACTICE INDICATORS

In working with self-injury and self-harm in counselling and psychotherapy, there are a number of therapist qualities that, if in place, help contribute to ethical, sensitive and responsive therapy that also attends to the possibility of risk. I have outlined these qualities elsewhere (Reeves, 2013a: 33–4), but revisit them here:

- Any counsellor must be qualified (or in advanced training) and drawing on a core theoretical model (or integration of models) to support their practice.
- Regular supervision must be in place, meeting at least the minimum requirements of supervision set by relevant professional bodies.

- The counsellor must work within the context of a clear ethical framework.
- Any counselling must be carefully contracted, including clearly setting boundaries around time, availability between sessions and confidentiality.
- The counsellor must be a reflective practitioner, with a willingness to identify professional and personal areas for development and to seek resources to support that development, as appropriate.
- The counsellor must be able to engage with a dialogue around risk and be aware of any existing policies or procedures (where they exist) and work accordingly.
- The counsellor needs to make him- or herself aware of issues around self-injury and self-harm, including: types of self-injury and self-harm; why people might hurt themselves; the consequences of self-injury and self-harm for the client and those around them; and what the research tells us about self-injury and self-harm; and be willing to explore their own strategies for coping under stress, which might include forms of self-injury or self-harm.
- The counsellor must be willing to communicate clearly with clients about the client's self-injury or self-harm.
- The counsellor must be aware of the danger of becoming self-injury or self-harm focused, where this is not the client's wish or goal while, at the same time, being mindful of the risk that might be present.
- The counsellor must not judge, but must be empathic, compassionate and understanding, and willing to be congruent (in line with the teachings of their core theoretical framework).
- The counsellor must be willing to name risk as it presents, and to work proactively and collaboratively with clients to engage with the risk in a way that is respectful of the client's wellbeing and autonomy, where possible.

Chapter summary

In this chapter we have considered some of the definitions of self-harm and their implications for practice. More specifically, we have differentiated between self-injury and self-harm (providing examples of each) and outlined why such a differentiation can be helpful when working with aspects of risk. Using two case scenarios, we have looked at ways in which risk might present when working with self-injury with a client, and then with self-harm, and ways in which the therapist might explore concerns with clients so that risk is fully acknowledged and engaged with.

6

THE DANGER OF VIOLENCE AND HARM TO OTHERS

Chapter outline

Suicide and self-injury/harm are often the central focus of a practitioner's concern, with generally less attention focused on harm to others. This includes emotional harm (such as threats, manipulation or coercion), as well as physical harm. How risk of violence might present in the therapeutic process, as well as in relationships beyond therapy, will be explored. Key research will be highlighted as well as known indicators for potential violence.

INTRODUCTION

Risk of violence to others is something we all talk about, but also rarely talk about. The contradiction in this sentence is not an error in writing, but rather explains our response to the risk of violence to others in our assessment in counselling and psychotherapy. If I deconstruct the contradiction to illustrate what I mean: we all talk about the risk of violence because it is something that is included in the majority of contracts for therapy we agree. We will say something about confidentiality being limited if we have immediate concerns about 'harm to the client or someone else'. While 'harm to someone else' can also include child protection, which I will discuss in more detail in the next chapter, it also refers to the risk of our clients harming another person and that, if we suspect that is an immediate reality, we might need to act to protect the other person. That we rarely talk about it derives from the fact that so little is written specifically for counsellors and psychotherapists to help them with that assessment; there is a dearth of information that really informs our practice and helps us to understand what, exactly, we should be looking for.

This presents a real challenge to the contracts we make. While the concept of duty of care is a difficult one to really pin down, it would be fair to say that we have a duty of care in our contracts to be competent and willing to do the things we say we are going to do. I'm not aware of research that considers how assessing risk of violence is taught on therapy training programmes in the UK. Anecdotally, having asked around a large number of colleagues, I have not yet found anyone who had specific time during their training to consider such risks. My suspicion is that it is not something that is widely addressed in training and yet the overwhelming majority of us will contract with our clients to act in the event of such concerns.

The phrase 'violence to others' is additionally problematic in that it is an ill-defined term that is potentially quite wide ranging. The presumption is often that 'violence' would refer to physical violence and thus physical harm, whereas we know from evidence (Follingstad and Rogers, 2014; NSPCC, 2014a) (and our own experiences with clients) the destructive nature of emotional violence – or 'harm' – and the impact it can have on people. As practitioners we therefore need to be clear as to what we mean by 'violence or harm to someone', what the risk indicators might be, how we might identify them in sessions and what we would do if we did.

DEFINING VIOLENCE AND HARM

The *Oxford English Dictionary* (2014) defines violence as: 'The exercise of physical force so as to inflict injury on, or cause damage to, persons or property; action or conduct characterised by this; treatment or usage tending to cause bodily injury.' While 'harm' is defined as: 'to injure (physically or otherwise); to hurt, damage'. From these two definitions we can see that violence is generally defined more in terms of a physical action leading to a physical negative consequence, whereas harm is a broader term that would include actions beyond the specific nature of violence, but also including violence, such as emotional harm, for example.

These are interesting points as they raise immediate questions about the nature and extent of the contracts we agree with our clients. When we limit confidentiality if we suspect the immediate risk of violence to another that might mean something slightly different from occasions when we suspect the immediate risk of harm to another. One is potentially more specific, while the other a little more inclusive. Certainly, regardless of the actual terms used in the contracting process, we need to ensure we are transparent with our clients about what we mean so they fully understand the boundaries and limitations of what we are able to hear confidentially.

The potential for violence and harm might present in therapy in many different ways, all of which require commensurate consideration on behalf of the therapist about what that might mean in relation to the therapeutic process, but also the boundaries of confidentiality agreed. It is difficult to provide a complete and definitive list of potential violence and harm, as there are so many different ways in which it might present, but a number of risks associated with violence and harm might include:

- Threat of or actual physical injury or harm to another adult, known or unknown to the client
- Threat of or actual physical injury or harm to another adult in the family setting (domestic or family violence)
- Threat of or actual physical injury or harm to a child or young person (triggering child protection concerns)
- Threat of or actual physical injury or harm to the therapist
- Threat of or actual sexual violence or exploitation of another
- Threat of or actual financial exploitation of another
- Threat of or actual emotional exploitation or coercion of another
- An act of terrorism.

What becomes apparent in the examples above is that focusing our definition on the potential for violence could inadvertently lead us to disregard other areas for potential harm that might trigger an intervention. It is my suggestion that it is more helpful to work with the concept of harm to another, which is inclusive of actual or potential violence, as a term that encompasses the wide range of issues that can present in therapy. However, working with the concept of harm does not, in itself, make the process of knowing what to do any easier. Consider the brief scenario about Adrien below.

The potential for harm: Adrien

Adrien is a 28-year-old male client who is attending counselling because of problems with anger. He has been working well and feels that he is more able to manage his anger now. During a session however, he says something that makes you concerned. On asking him about this he tells you, because he knows 'this session is confidential', that he has been involved for a while in a gang that exploits 16- and 17-year-old young women and passes them on to his 'clients' for sex. While he knows this is wrong, it is also financially lucrative and he suspects that the young girls involved are 'probably quite happy deep down' to be involved too.

This scenario with Adrien highlights some of the very difficult dilemmas we might face in therapy: a client who brings their own understanding about the nature of the confidential relationship; the disclosure of wrongdoing; evidence of sexual and financial exploitation of vulnerable people; and a created rationale about the young girls' willingness to be involved, thus a mitigation of personal responsibility for his action, for example. Suddenly Adrien's therapist is propelled into a difficult situation about how best to respond to Adrien and whether they should pass on their concerns, and if so, to whom.

Pause for reflection

1 What do you consider are the key areas of concern with respect to violence and harm here?
2 What do you think are the therapist's priorities in responding to Adrien: (a) therapeutically; and (b) in relation to confidentiality?
3 What would you do, and what would be your reasons for your actions?

There are very few situations beyond the risk of terrorism where we are duty bound under law to disclose the risk of harm, and yet we might make decisions to do so on the grounds of 'public interest'. This is the case with suicide risk, where there is no statutory obligation to pass on concerns about potential suicide, but where we instead take a moral and ethical position about the best interests of the client. As we can see, while there is a legal safeguard to disclose personal information about a client, if necessary and in exceptional circumstances without their consent, on the grounds of public interest, the concept of public interest does not, in itself, define those circumstances beyond the risk of harm to others or society. Inherent in this difficulty is the extent and nature of the harm we suspect and our own assessment, informed by many factors, of the harm.

What is important here is that we take time to carefully consider what we mean by harm and the points at which we might need to consider disclosing the potential for harm; in short, what exactly do we mean by 'harm to others' when we use that term to potentially limit confidentiality in our contracting? There are a number of factors that will inform our understanding of harm and how we might act in accordance with the contracts we make with clients, including:

- *The age and demographic profile of the clients we work with*: such as whether our clients are children or young people, or cultural aspects
- *The organisational context of therapy*: the organisation's relationship to harm, such as the differences between working in statutory settings, the third sector, independent practice or in a prison setting, for example
- *Any policies or procedures at an organisational level that inform practice decisions*: how harm might be defined organisationally and any expectations of practitioners
- *Legal parameters, such as terrorism and capacity, for example*: if the law directs us to act in any particular way
- *Our own experience of harm, both professionally and personally*: personal or professional experiences will shape our attitudes to harm
- *Our tolerance towards risk*: whether we are risk averse or risk tolerant, and where we are on that continuum in any given scenario
- *Our wider views about the nature of harm and its implications*: including our own moral and social 'positioning' in relation to harm, such as drug use or prostitution, for example
- *Discussions in supervision*: all these aspects will apply to our supervisor too, so clarity about supervisory expectations of good practice.

It is important that these points are carefully considered, preferably prior to a situation arising, so that all the implications of the therapeutic contract and what it might mean in practice have been carefully considered, thus minimising the danger of reactive practice.

ASSESSING FOR RISK OF HARM

Like working with suicide risk, there are a number of questionnaires and risk assessment approaches developed to look specifically at risk of harm to others, such as the Violence Risk Assessment Guide (VRAG – for more information about this see Quinsey et al., 1998) and the Risk Management Assessment Scheme (HCR-20 – for more information about this see Douglas et al., 1999). However, these have generally been designed by other disciplines, such as social work and psychiatry, so their transferability into the counselling and psychotherapy world is not so clear. Some tools already used in therapy, such as CORE-OM, include a statement about harm to others and that can be a useful way of opening a discussion, whether or not the client has responded positively to it (i.e. indicating some threatening or intimidating behaviour to others in the last week). A number of factors have been determined to have some predictive power as to whether or not a person is likely to act on their thoughts of harm.

Newhill (2014: 3) outlines a number of indicators for potential harm:

Demographic

- Young age
- Male (but not always).

Clinical

- High-risk psychiatric symptoms (delusions, hallucinations, violent fantasies)
- Personality features (anger, emotional dysregulation, impulsivity)
- Personality disorder (antisocial, borderline)
- Substance abuse (alcohol and drug use).

Biological

- Neurological impairment
- Organic disorders.

Historical

- History of violence (recentness and frequency of self-reports of violence toward others, arrests, incarcerations, and reports of violence toward self)
- Social and family history (early exposure to violence)
- Work history (economic instability, unemployment)
- History of psychiatric treatment and hospitalisation.

Environmental/contextual

- Level and quality of social support
- Peer pressure from peers who endorse violence
- Influence of popular culture
- Means for violence (access to lethal weapons and knowledge of how to use them)
- Potential victims that are accessible.

Additionally, Niolon (2006: 1) provides some key considerations that are helpful to keep in mind when thinking about the potential for harm. He says that it is important to remember that:

- almost anyone, under the right circumstances, can become violent
- most of the time, violence is the response of a person who feels that all other options are exhausted, and there is nothing to gain by restraining themselves and nothing to lose by becoming violent
- the reasoning and self-control that hinder the person from choosing this 'last response' are likely to be weakened by substance use, mental illness (ranging from severe depression to delusional thinking), and severe stress
- this 'last response' is often accompanied by a strong feeling of helplessness and powerlessness, and violence is seen as a way to increase control and influence in the situation
- when helplessness is not the predominant emotion, fear of harm or exploitation is the next most likely one.

Niolson offers a useful mnemonic to help remember the key factors: TMAPP – T: thoughts of harming another; M: means to harm another; A: access to means to harm another; P: pervasive thoughts of causing harm to another; and P: plans to harm another. It seems therefore, that the potential for harm to another is likely to be increased where:

- There is ideation of harm, or an intention to act on thoughts of harming another
- The client is highly distressed and feels 'backed into a corner' by a situation
- The client lacks empathy for the other and cannot see the consequences of their potential actions on the other
- There are factors that might otherwise diminish inhibitions against anger, such as alcohol, drug use, severe mental health distress, organic or physical disorders (e.g. head injury)
- They have learnt that violence is an accepted form of communication (e.g. family violence, or gang culture)
- The client lacks affective control (i.e. struggles to contain impulsive reactions, or reacts quickly and without thought in situations).

Some of these factors might be classed as *interpersonal*, in that they refer to how the client relates to others and their experiences, both historical and current, and how others have related to them; and some are *intrapersonal*, in that they refer to how the client relates to themselves, their conceptualisation of the situation and their capacity to empathise. The inter- and intrapersonal aspects of exploration are important when evaluating the potential for harm in therapy. Despenser (2005: 439) reflects on how we, as therapists, might engage with these aspects from a therapeutic position, rather than just through the identification of key factors. She notes the following three areas:

- *Signposts in client's history*: reported episodes of violence or aggression (ideas and actions), psychiatric and forensic history, self-harm, abuse, use of medication. Some of this information might be contained in a referral letter, otherwise it is gathered in first session/s.
- *Signposts in client's initial, current and ongoing state*: including evidence at any time of erratic state or intoxication, body language, verbal clues, recent or anticipated changes in client's situation or support network, ego strength.
  - o An example was given of a verbal clue that led to termination of the contract with a male client: *'Aren't you afraid, working down the end of this corridor at night?'* (Despenser, 2005: 439)
  - o Examples of body language included overt sexual posturing. Two participants, commenting on cases where they initially felt intimidated by a client's physical size and dress, remarked that they would attempt not to judge the situation solely on appearances.
- Clues in countertransference feelings throughout the work, from first hearing the client's voice. Terminology included: 'gut reaction', 'all antennae active', 'instinct'.

In the exploratory stage of looking at the potential for harm it is important that we feel confident to ask specific questions of the client to help: (a) gather key information in relation to identifying risk factors; and (b) provide a space for exploration. If we note one of the factors listed above, that the client cannot see an alternative to their situation and feels 'backed into a corner', the space to honestly and openly explore their feelings can help to mitigate the risk. As the client is able to feel heard and understood they are provided with an opportunity to think of alternative mechanisms for expressing their feelings. However, the concept of immediacy is important here in determining the usefulness of such exploration. The degree to which the risk is immediate, or deferred, is helpful to consider: a deferred risk (something that I have thoughts of doing but with no immediate intention) provides the scope for empathic exploration with a view to help reduce the risk through the identification of alternative actions; an immediate risk is less open to exploration (although this is not impossible) and rather the danger as it presents must be responded to in a calm and safe way. In this context we must always be sensitive to our own capacity to engage in such discussions. If we feel frightened of the client, perhaps because of the danger in the room, we must always respect that and find ways in which we can either decrease the danger, or end the session and seek help. We must therefore keep the following parameters in mind:

- Whether the risk of harm is immediate or deferred
- Whether the risk of harm is impulsive or planned
- Whether the risk of harm is towards the therapist in the room, or another outside of the therapy setting
- Whether the client has the capacity and willingness to talk about the potential risk
- Whether the therapist has the capacity and willingness to talk about the potential risk.

Pause for reflection

1 How might you feel about talking to a client about their potential harm to others?
2 What are the factors that would make this easier to do, or more difficult to do?
3 For those factors that would make such a discussion harder to do, are there any steps you might take to deal with this (e.g. discussions in supervision, health and safety arrangements in your workplace, etc.)?

PERSONAL SAFETY

Even though occurrences of therapists being assaulted by their clients are fortunately rare, the need to pay due regard to health and safety considerations remains an imperative. If we keep in mind the idea that anyone is capable of inflicting harm on another and that our actions should always take that possibility into account, we take important steps towards protecting our own safety. Certainly, the occasions when I have been threatened by violence in a meeting with a client have occurred with people I knew well and already had an established relationship with; their deteriorating mental health distress was a trigger for their actions. Assuming the potential for risk in all situations also helps to mitigate the danger of acting on discriminatory or stereotypical views of people who we believe, without evidence, are more inclined towards violence than others.

There are general ways in which we can help to protect our clients, and ourselves, and actions that might be required in specific threatening situations.

General considerations

While the following actions do not, in themselves, prevent violence or harm to others, they do provide a good practice context in which the danger can be at least mitigated. Such steps might include:

- Ensuring health and safety is fully and proactively attended to
- Ensuring policies and working procedures are in place that specifically address safety concerns so that both the practitioner and client are protected
- In organisational settings, ensuring that 'lone worker' policies (i.e. that prohibit workers seeing clients alone in buildings, etc.) or 'checking in' procedures are in place and understood by all concerned, as well as reviewing those policies regularly
- In independent practice, giving thought as to how safety can be managed, such as ensuring there are 'contact points' with people throughout the day, or that systems are in place to summon help if needed (e.g. personal alarms, telephone contact, etc.)
- Ensuring that third party referrers are asked about the potential for harm to others at the point of referral
- If personal alarms are available, ensuring they are always accessible
- Where possible and if there is a choice, ensuring you sit nearest the door, rather than the client becoming a barrier between you and a means of escape
- If using stairs, leading a client up the stairs and following them down
- Ensuring that early assessments, or exploration of goals and hopes for therapy, openly and honestly explore the potential for harm to others
- Checking that the working contract fully addresses the potential for harm to others and the actions to be taken in the event of concerns
- Ensuring that the client and therapist fully understand the implications of the therapeutic contract for practice
- Taking time to talk through in supervision issues surrounding harm to others and what actions might be taken in which circumstances
- Ensuring that any concerns are carefully recorded so that these can be fully addressed in supervision, and so that they can be clearly communicated to others if a further referral is required.

Specific actions if under threat

As has been stated, while the circumstances are rare it is important that practitioners know and keep in mind steps they might take if faced with an angry or threatening client to try to reduce the levels of risk and de-escalate the situation so that help can be summoned. Niolon (2006: 3–4) notes that the following can help to prevent the possibility of a physical attack:

- Remain calm at all times, speaking in a soft and gentle voice
- Validate the client's feelings using short, clear and accessible statements
- Mirroring body posture, such as using empathic nods and non-verbal acknowledgements
- Acknowledging any feelings they may have that relate to unfairness and prejudice
- Avoid contradicting the client or taking a position of power over them; aim for the relationship to remain equal and calm
- Pay attention to your own feelings so that you can keep calm, even if this might prove difficult
- Regulate your own breathing so that it is calm, and avoid quick movements or movements towards the client
- Don't turn your back on the client and, if possible, remain in a 45 degrees position to them (rather than face to face) to avoid the client interpreting your position as confrontative
- Remember that our personal space increases when under threat: be respectful of your client's personal space and, if possible, move away slightly
- Try to shift any discussion towards problem-solving: the progress they have already made (for a new client attending counselling), what would make things better now and how might they be supported to achieve their goals
- Do not interrupt or challenge the client if they are 'venting' their anger verbally. Allow this process to happen and then, when the client is ready, offer the opportunity to talk about the points they have made. Verbal expression of anger, if facilitated, can often prevent physical expressions of anger
- Help the client increase self-awareness around their escalating behaviour by bringing it gently but firmly to their attention, 'I can see Joyce that you are becoming quite angry and upset as we talk about this. I am concerned about you and am here to help, but we must both be safe while we do that', for example
- Do not promise actions that you cannot deliver – always be honest and realistic about what you can do
- Don't be anxious about bringing the session to a close if the client does not calm down, either, 'I think we will need to end this session now as I am concerned about how angry you are', or 'perhaps if we took a short break so we can have time to think, and then meet again in a few minutes'
- Do not try to restrain the client and, if they wish to leave the room, allow them to do so
- If the client makes further threats or appears to ready themselves to attack you, leave the room if possible and call for help.

It is my own experience from practice that the majority of clients, even when highly distressed and agitated, can, with a calm, empathic, reassuring and respectful manner, be supported so that the situation is de-escalated. Careful assessment in the early stages of counselling and attention paid to the nature of the contract can help prevent such situations arising.

AN ETHICAL CONUNDRUM: WHAT SHOULD WE DO?

It is difficult in the majority of situations to give clear advice as to how you should respond to situations where risk of harm to someone else is suspected or likely. As we have explored throughout this chapter, the concept of harm is sufficiently broad to encompass a full range of actions and our responses as therapists will, in turn, be informed by a number of other factors, such as the setting in which therapy takes place, the relationship with the client, the contract agreed with the client, policies and procedures, the capacity and willingness of the client to work with the issues, including their level of insight, and so on. Most importantly, each of us needs to be clear as to what would be the boundaries of our confidentiality so that these can be clearly explained to clients.

Public interest actions, whereby we act on a reasonable belief to safeguard the wellbeing of society or individuals, are defensible in law but must be taken with careful thought and attention to the available information. We need to be able to recognise the factors that might make risk of harm more likely, protective factors that might make the risk less likely, and the client's capacity and willingness to not act on their thoughts. We need additionally to determine whether the client is exploring more general ideation ('Sometimes I just really want to hit them, but I wouldn't do it'), or has an expressed intent ('That person is going to get what they deserve'), a deferred idea ('I can see myself blowing up at some point and doing something') or a more immediate plan ('I've had enough. I'm going to go and see them now and sort this out').

The following is offered as very general guidance and should not be applied strictly in all situations, but can be a useful structure in which to consider responses:

- *Ideation and deferred plan*: explore the client's thoughts and feelings and help them consider ways in which they may be able to express their feelings safely, while reminding them of the boundaries of confidentiality and your concern to help protect their own and others' wellbeing. Discuss in supervision and with line manager or colleagues.
- *Intent and deferred plan:* continue to explore the client's thoughts and feelings and help them to consider ways in which they may be able to

express their feelings safely. Remind the client of your commitment to their own and others' wellbeing and of the priority to ensure they do not act on their thoughts. Remind them of the boundaries of confidentiality and your concern to help protect their own and others' wellbeing. Discuss in supervision and with line manager or colleagues.

- *Intent and immediate plan*: if you have reason to believe that your client has an immediate intention to harm another person you must inform your client about the contract that gives a commitment to the safety and wellbeing of them, and others. And that in harming someone else they will also be harming themselves. Ask for their consent to seek additional help and, if consent is obtained, do so. If consent is refused consider a public interest disclosure of concern, preferably following immediate consultation with a supervisor or line manager. This might involve ringing the police, or the client's GP if you suspect your client is experiencing mental health distress.

By virtue of the context of counselling and psychotherapy, it is likely that the client will be experiencing significant emotional turmoil in their lives. Given the propensity for the client's actions to be shaped by their mental health distress, disclosure of concerns is best made in the first instance to the client's GP (with the client's permission, wherever possible, but without it if need be). The discussion with the GP can help share responsibility for action and determine the best sort of action required. This might be the involvement of the police, or rather of a statutory Mental Health Act assessment, particularly if the client is known to the GP or mental health services. However, it may be that immediate contact with the police is required for public protection. This may be because of discussions with the client's GP or, if the client's GP is not available, following discussions with a supervisor and/or line manager, or if the urgency of the situation is deemed to require it. If this is undertaken the following information should be provided:

- The client's name, age, gender and culture
- Any identifying features, plus what the client was wearing on leaving the session
- The client's home address, or the address of any other key person involved
- Who you are and why you are ringing
- The specific nature of the risk: what the client said, what they intend to do, who is being threatened or why you believe there is a risk
- Any additional relevant information, *without* passing on personal information explored in counselling that should remain confidential. The only information disclosed should be to enable the police to do their job and safeguard the client's and others' immediate safety.

Often the anxiety such situations arouse is exacerbated by not knowing what to do. The above points are simply general indicators of good practice and may differ in your particular working contexts. Use the above ideas as a starting point for discussion about your own preferred responses.

Chapter summary

In this chapter we have acknowledged that while we all contract around concerns of risk to others, very little is written for counsellors and psychotherapists specifically to help them to respond to such concerns. In contracting boundaries of confidentiality limited by risk of harm to others, it is important that we know what we mean, what we are looking for and how we might respond in such situations.

In looking at the definitions we considered how the term 'violence' is often used to mean physical threat or action, whereas the term 'harm' is more inclusive of the types of situations that might more typically present in therapy. We have considered a number of key risk factors for increased potential of harm to others, including demographic, contextual, historical and emotional/psychological. Additionally, we considered a number of useful questions therapists might keep in mind when thinking about risk to others.

Finally, we considered steps that therapists might take in the event of concern and how they should consult, wherever possible, before breaking a client's confidentiality. We acknowledged that there are some limited circumstances where we might need to make public interest decisions, to safeguard the wellbeing of the client or others, but that such decisions should be based on a carefully thought out rationale informed by the available information that indicated risk. In this context, we also acknowledged the importance of using the therapeutic space to explore issues of risk as part of the therapeutic process. Finally, we identified key information to keep in mind in responding to risk, including direct risk of harm to the therapist.

7

SAFEGUARDING AND CHILD PROTECTION

Chapter outline

While many organisations have clear policies on how risk to young people should be responded to, the reality is that many counsellors and psychotherapists remain uncertain when and how to respond to safeguarding concerns. This chapter will consider what is meant by safeguarding and child protection, the legal aspects that inform practice around working with safeguarding concerns and some good practice indicators for working proactively with risk in this area.

INTRODUCTION

It is not uncommon for discussions around counselling and psychotherapy in the context of safeguarding to lead to high levels of anxiety and concern. Over the years I have spoken with many therapists who work with children, young people and vulnerable adults and they often cite safeguarding as their biggest worry: what it means, their responsibilities and what if things should go wrong. Certainly the spectre of the failure to protect a child or young person from harm is never far away, with regular media reports highlighting the tragic consequences of when things do go wrong. While these accounts are indeed dreadful they do not highlight the many thousands of children and young people who are protected and safeguarded each year through the application of good practice and grounded pragmatism. By 'grounded pragmatism', I mean the application of policies, procedures and good practice in the context of real-world settings and all the uncertainties and unpredictable aspects that go with that. Like all areas of risk in therapy, issues around safeguarding and child protection are fraught with the lack of certainty about what might happen 'if'. Regardless of how carefully we work with a situation we can never accurately predict its outcome, but simply use all available information wisely and work within the parameters of guidance and accepted good practice.

In this chapter we will try to unpack these concepts a little more. The term 'safeguarding' is now used extensively and yet we do not often sit down and really consider what it means. Likewise, the term 'child protection' does not fully articulate the complexity of a process that is underpinned by a legislative frame. Often we also imagine that safeguarding applies to children and young people, whereas it applies to vulnerable adults too. It can certainly be a complex area and the anxieties it provokes are often understandable. However, like working with suicide risk, or self-injury, or severe mental health deterioration, it is eminently possible to work ethically and to a high standard within the context of risk, as long as we do so transparently, collaboratively (wherever possible and appropriate), consistently, responsively, and are prepared to act when we no longer feel that the risk is safely or appropriately contained in the context of therapy.

SAFEGUARDING

While many might see safeguarding as a professional responsibility, which it is, it cannot be located only in that frame. Guidance around safeguarding makes it clear from the outset that it is everyone's responsibility. While there is a responsibility that is enshrined in law and brings with it certain tasks and duties to particular professional groups, beyond that the concept of safeguarding is one that is applicable to all: we all have a duty as citizens and members of a society to attend to the care and wellbeing of those vulnerable groups within it. By vulnerable groups we mean those people who – through age, emotional or mental capacity or competence, or illness or disability – are more vulnerable to harm and exploitation. The societal responsibility here is not only to ensure that we do not act in such a way as to bring about harm, but also that we also act to help protect vulnerable people from harm when it is suspected or apparent.

Here we will consider safeguarding. It is interesting to note that many conflate the terms safeguarding and child protection to mean the same things, whereas child protection is a specific aspect of safeguarding but does not, in and of itself, incorporate the wider conceptual ideas that relate to safeguarding. In essence, child protection is about assessment and intervention to protect children from harm, while safeguarding is about not only protection from harm but also promotion of wellbeing and good outcomes for all vulnerable people – a much more proactive concept.

Children and young people

The concept of safeguarding as it applies to children and guidance (HM Government, 2013: 7) is:

- Protecting children from maltreatment;
- Preventing impairment of children's health or development;
- Ensuring that children grow up in circumstances consistent with the provision of safe and effective care; and
- Taking action to enable all children to have the best outcomes.

As we can see from this definition, safeguarding not only refers to protecting children and young people from harm but also actively promoting their wellbeing. As such, safeguarding procedures, usually in places that attend to children and young peoples' needs (such as schools, youth services – including counselling and psychotherapy services), look towards the ways in which children and young people can be protected from harm and how the delivery of their services can promote wellbeing and the 'best outcomes', such as educational, pastoral, emotional, psychological and physical outcomes, for example, and are overseen by Local Safeguarding Children Boards (LSCBs – established by the Children Act, 2004). Given that the assumption in UK guidance is that safeguarding is best achieved when people are clear as to their own particular responsibilities, the importance of clear and accessible procedures becomes apparent. Guidance (HM Government, 2013: 7–8) recommends that effective safeguarding systems are those where:

- the child's needs are paramount, and the needs and wishes of each child, be they a baby or infant, or an older child, should be put first, so that every child receives the support they need before a problem escalates
- all professionals who come into contact with children and families are alert to their needs and any risks of harm that individual abusers, or potential abusers, may pose to children

- all professionals share appropriate information in a timely way and can discuss any concerns about an individual child with colleagues and local authority children's social care
- high quality professionals are able to use their expert judgement to put the child's needs at the heart of the safeguarding system so that the right solution can be found for each individual child
- all professionals contribute to whatever actions are needed to safeguard and promote a child's welfare and take part in regularly reviewing the outcomes for the child against specific plans and outcomes.

The points above are worthy but in some ways also challenge the traditional model of counselling and psychotherapy and how it translates to the provision of services to children and young people. If we take two of the above points and consider them in a little more detail:

All professionals share appropriate information in a timely way and can discuss any concerns about an individual child with colleagues and local authority children's social care

Counselling and psychotherapy has, for many decades, been structured around a very particular form of confidentiality. The level of trust between the client and therapist, and the development of an effective and facilitative therapeutic alliance is grounded on the principle that, apart from exceptional circumstances, what is said between client and therapist is confidential to that relationship. As therapy has moved into new contexts practitioners have had to wrestle with the application of confidentiality when working in a multi-disciplinary way. How do we protect the privacy of our clients while working effectively with others for the overall wellbeing of the client? As the guidance states:

> No single professional can have a full picture of a child's needs and circumstances and, if children and families are to receive the right help at the right time, everyone who comes into contact with them has a role to play in identifying concerns, sharing information and taking prompt action. (HM Government: 2013: 8)

This is one of the areas of practice that causes therapists some of the anxiety we talked about earlier: the capacity to work confidentially with children and young people in therapy while, at the same time, being mindful of safeguarding procedures and expectations of action. Alongside this, are the implications of Gillick competence and the Fraser Guidelines, which we will explore in a little more detail later in the chapter. In summary, therapists need to find a way of agreeing a contract of confidentiality with children and young people that promotes trust and the development of the alliance while, at the same time, being mindful of safeguarding expectations that will require them to work collaboratively with other professionals, sharing information as and when required. Meeting the needs of children and young people is a complex matter given that there will be occasions when the actions required will go against the wishes of the young person.

High-quality professionals are able to use their expert judgement to put the child's needs at the heart of the safeguarding system so that the right solution can be found for each individual child

This principle places a challenge on therapists to be able to explicitly and judiciously use their knowledge and skills to make informed decisions about children and young people with regard to risk. We have discussed in earlier chapters the challenge inherent in this task, given that risk is often about using the best information available in the context of uncertainty and unpredictability. As much as we try, we can rarely predict an outcome, but rather make a best judgement on the likelihood of an outcome and act accordingly. In this context the challenge is for therapists to be able to recognise: (a) when a child or young person's needs can be safely contained in the therapeutic frame; (b) when the continued provision of therapy will be of benefit to the child or young person, but in the context of additional support; and (c) when the risk of harm to the child or young person is such that referral on to other services for assessment and intervention is required, if necessary without the child or young person's consent (although with it, if at all possible). We will revisit these issues later in the chapter. Consider the scenario of Martin.

Safeguarding children and young people: Martin

Martin is 12 years old and has been referred to the school counsellor by his class teacher. Martin has been getting into fights with other boys and has been increasingly abusive to the class teacher. The school have little contact with his family, but are aware that his behaviour is now different to how he was in primary school. Martin likes counselling as he feels he can talk. He tells his counsellor, Judy, that his mum and dad have separated. He is pleased about that because he would often see his dad shouting and being angry at his mum. Seeing these events made him frightened and upset and he doesn't want his dad to come back. Martin does not want Judy to tell the school about this.

There are potential child protection aspects here that Judy might need to explore further, such as whether Martin's dad ever acted that way against him or physically hurt him. Additionally, the potential for emotional harm through witnessing such incidents must be considered. In terms of safeguarding Judy must attend to Martin's wellbeing and ensure that his needs remain a priority. This situation encapsulates the common dilemma of how best to meet a child's needs: in this case, should Judy raise concerns with the school so that family interventions might be put in place, but in doing so against Martin's wishes, potentially rupture the therapeutic alliance; or should she respect Martin's wish for confidentiality, certainly at this stage, acknowledging that he finds counselling helpful and is able to talk freely about his worries.

Pause for reflection

1 What do you consider are the factors that would point Judy to the first course of action: passing on concerns to the school, against Martin's wishes?

2 What do you consider are the factors that would point Judy to the second course of action: respecting Martin's wishes around confidentiality at this stage and continue to work with him without raising concerns with the school?

3 What would you do, and what would be your reasons?

Vulnerable adults

Similar principles apply in the safeguarding of vulnerable adults, but obviously with a slightly different focus given the demographic differences. The term 'vulnerable adults' refers to people over the age of 18, with safeguarding for children and young people applying up to the age of 18. A definition of a vulnerable adult was issued in a 1997 consultation paper (DoH and Home Office, 2000: 8–9; see also Lord Chancellor's Department, 1997, 1999) that was broadly inclusive, and stated that a 'vulnerable adult':

is a person who may be in need of community care services by reason of mental or other disability, age or illness; and who is or may be unable to take care of him or herself, or unable to protect him or herself against significant harm or exploitation.

The term 'community care services' refers to 'all care services provided in any setting or context' (2000: 9), which would include the provision of psychological care services such as counselling and psychotherapy, although while not all clients would fall into the definition of 'vulnerable adult', the potential for them doing so is important to keep in mind.

The guidance acknowledges that the term 'abuse' can mean a variety of things and offers a further broad statement when it suggests that abuse is, 'a violation of an individual's human and civil rights by any other person or persons' (2000: 9), but then offers a more detailed account of the types of abuse that would be addressed under safeguarding procedures (2000: 9):

- *Physical abuse*: hitting, slapping, pushing, kicking, misuse of medication, restraint or inappropriate sanctions
- *Sexual abuse*: including rape and sexual assault or sexual acts to which the vulnerable adult has not consented, or could not consent or was pressurised into consenting
- *Psychological abuse*: including emotional abuse, threats of harm or abandonment, deprivation of contact, humiliation, blaming, controlling, intimidation, coercion, harassment, verbal abuse, isolation, or withdrawal from services or supportive networks
- *Financial or material abuse*: including theft, fraud, exploitation, pressure in connection with wills, property or inheritance or financial transactions, or the misuse or misappropriation of property, possessions or benefits
- *Neglect and acts of omission*: including ignoring medical or physical care needs, failure to provide access to appropriate health, social care or educational services, the withholding of the necessities of life, such as medication, adequate nutrition and heating
- *Discriminatory abuse*: including racist, sexist, that based on a person's disability, and other forms of harassment, slurs or similar treatment.

It is worth noting that some of the above elements would also fall into the category of criminal behaviour, such as rape or physical assault, while others might be harder to categorise, such as controlling and coercion. Of course, someone might perpetrate instances of abuse in a professional caring role, other official or professional role, or might be a friend, family member or a stranger, and instances of abuse can happen in any context. As was discussed in Chapter 6 about harm to others, we should assume that everyone has the potential to be harmed (even if we don't assume that everyone *is* being harmed).

Making decisions about when and how to intervene is a complex process that will be informed by many factors. In general terms the guidance (DoH and Home Office, 2000: 12–13) outlines the following parameters that professionals should use to inform their thinking about interventions:

- The vulnerability of the individual
- The nature and extent of the abuse
- The length of time it has been occurring
- The impact on the individual
- The risk of repeated or increasingly serious acts involving this individual or other vulnerable adults.

When thinking about counselling and psychotherapy services specifically, I would add the following points to consider:

- The wishes of the client, in the context of their mental capacity (whether they are able to make informed decisions about their wellbeing at that time)
- The context in which therapy is taking place
- The contract of confidentiality agreed with the client
- Any policies or procedures in place to inform practice in such situations
- The ethical framework within which the practitioner operates
- The theoretical orientation of the practitioner (where the focus on client autonomy is greater than in other approaches, for example)
- Balancing the risk of intervention against the risk of non-intervention.

While the challenges are slightly different when thinking about safeguarding vulnerable adults as opposed to children and young people, the approach is the same: keeping in mind the client's known wishes (if they have the capacity to make informed decisions at that stage), the contract of therapy and the potential for risk of harm. Consider the scenario with Alice.

Safeguarding vulnerable adults: Alice

Alice is 78 years old and has been attending counselling in a third sector setting with Janine, following a hospital discharge; she remains physically frail. Since her partner died four years previously she has lived alone, supported by her daughter who lives locally. Alice has never really got on well with her daughter and describes her as 'bossy and likes to be in charge'. Alice struggles with financial problems and says this isn't helped by having to give her daughter over half her pension every month for looking after her. She insists that Janine does not tell anyone as it would only make matters worse, and that she hopes Janine will respect her decision about confidentiality as she has valued feeling equal and listened to in counselling.

According to the definition given above Alice would fall into the category of vulnerable adult by virtue of her age, physical health and general frailty. She is more susceptible to abuse given that she is less able to act to protect herself. In accordance with the scope of abuse outlined previously, there is strong evidence that Alice is being financially exploited by a 'bossy' daughter – who may also be coercing, controlling and bullying Alice. However, despite her physical frailty, Alice appears to have mental capacity – and the law makes adults with mental capacity free to make decisions for themselves, even if they are unwise. In this instance Alice has stated her wishes clearly for Janine to respect her confidentiality. However, Janine is also aware of the safeguarding issues that are present here. The organisation does not have a policy on safeguarding vulnerable adults.

Pause for reflection

1 What are the factors that would point Janine towards breaking Alice's confidentiality?
2 What are the factors that would point Janine to maintaining Alice's confidentiality?
3 What would you do, and what would be your reasons?

CHILD PROTECTION

Child protection legislation and practice vary slightly across England, Scotland, Northern Ireland and Wales. In England, the child protection legislative framework consists of the Children Act (1989) and the Children Act (2004). While many people believe there is a mandatory duty to report child protection concerns in England, this is not the case, although the majority of practitioners do have a duty to do so in virtue of LSCBs, or their employment responsibilities and the policies, procedures and guidance of professional bodies. There are some counselling and psychotherapy services that continue to offer absolute confidentiality around child protection on the basis that it provides a safe space for young people to talk about their experiences without fearing unwanted intervention. This is a moral and practice position and is entirely legal. It is worth noting that, at the time of writing, there is debate in England about whether or not the reporting of child protection concerns should be made mandatory.

Again, in Scotland there is no mandatory duty to report child protection concerns but there is an expectation that practitioners will do so. Child protection responsibility sits with the Scottish government. In Northern Ireland, Section 5(1) of the Criminal Law Act (1967) makes it a criminal offence to fail to report concerns related to child protection, distinguishing it from practice in England, Scotland and Wales. The responsibility for overseeing child protection is devolved to the Northern Ireland Executive and Northern Ireland government departments. In Wales, again there is no mandatory reporting requirement. How child protection services are structured in Wales may change as the Welsh Assembly is considering changes to legislation at the time of writing. More detailed information across the four regions can be downloaded from the NSPCC website (NSPCC, 2014b).

Child protection: defining abuse and indicators

There are four broad categories of child abuse that relate to child protection:

- Physical abuse
- Sexual abuse
- Emotional abuse
- Neglect.

The NSPCC (2014b) offers useful guidance to practitioners in recognising signs of abuse. General signs include:

- Regularly experiencing nightmares or sleeping problems.
- Changes in personality.
- Outbursts of anger.
- Changes in eating habits.
- Showing an inexplicable fear of particular places or making excuses to avoid particular people.
- Self-harming (includes head banging, scratching, cutting).
- Not receiving adequate medical attention after injuries.
- Showing violence to animals, toys, peers or adults.
- Knowledge of 'adult issues', e.g. alcohol, drugs, sexual behaviour.
- Lacking in confidence or often wary/anxious.
- Regressing to the behaviour of younger children.
- Regular flinching in response to sudden but harmless actions, e.g. someone raising a hand quickly.

They also offer specific potential indicators across different age ranges:

Infancy to preschool

- Doesn't cry or respond to parent's presence or absence from an early age (usually because they have learnt that their parent will not respond to their distress, this is known as a lack of attachment).
- Late in reaching developmental milestones such as learning to speak, with no medical reason.
- Acting out excessive violence with other children.
- Significantly underweight but eats well when given food.
- Talks of being left home alone or with strangers.

Middle childhood

- Talks of being left home alone or with strangers.
- Lacks social skills and has few if any friends.
- Shows lack of attachment to a parent.
- Becomes secretive and reluctant to share information.
- Acting out excessive violence with other children.

School age (5–16 years)

- Reluctant to go home after school.
- Unable to bring friends home or reluctant for professionals to visit the family home.
- Poor school attendance and punctuality, or late being picked up.
- Parents show little interest in child's performance and behaviour at school.
- Parents are dismissive and non-responsive to professional concerns.
- Is reluctant to get changed for PE, etc.
- Wets or soils the bed.
- Acting out excessive violence with other children.

Adolescence

- Drinks alcohol regularly from an early age.
- Is concerned for younger siblings without explaining why.
- Becomes secretive and reluctant to share information.
- Talks of running away.
- Shows challenging/disruptive behaviour at school.
- Is reluctant to get changed for PE, etc.

Unless you are based in a setting with a specific policy of absolute confidentiality around child protection you will almost certainly be expected by your employing organisation to act should there be concerns, preferably following consultation with a line manager and/ or supervisor, reporting concerns to the local social care services. If working independently you are free to define confidentiality arrangements as you see fit but must keep in mind guidance offered by professional bodies if you work within the scope of their ethical expectations.

GILLICK COMPETENCE AND THE FRASER GUIDELINES

The legal concept of Gillick competence and Fraser Guidelines comes from a legal hearing in the UK in 1982 when Victoria Gillick took her local health authority and the then Department of Health and Social Security to court in an attempt to prevent her daughter's GP from giving her contraceptive advice and treatment. Victoria Gillick argued that such treatment should only take place with parental consent for girls under the age of 16. Gillick's case was dismissed by the High Court, then reversed by the Court of Appeal but then the House of Lords affirmed the original ruling. In their statement they noted that:

> Whether or not a child is capable of giving the necessary consent will depend on the child's maturity and understanding and the nature of the consent required. The child must be capable of making a reasonable assessment of the advantages and disadvantages of the treatment proposed, so the consent, if given, can be properly and fairly described as true consent.

This was an important judgement because, while the original case referred specifically to the administering of contraception advice and treatment, the ruling introduced a broader concept of competence for young people under the age of 16 for making decisions for themselves. The Fraser Guidelines specifically refer to the guidelines given by Lord Fraser in his ruling on the original Gillick case. While these guidelines refer specifically to contraceptive advice to girls under the age of 16, the principles underpinning them have now been applied to a range of situations and are used to help guide decisions about a young person's competence to make decisions for themselves. The Fraser Guidelines specifically stated:

> a doctor could proceed to give advice and treatment provided he is satisfied in the following criteria:

1. that the girl (although under the age of 16 years of age) will understand his advice;
2. that he cannot persuade her to inform her parents or to allow him to inform the parents that she is seeking contraceptive advice;
3. that she is very likely to continue having sexual intercourse with or without contraceptive treatment;
4. that unless she receives contraceptive advice or treatment her physical or mental health or both are likely to suffer;
5. that her best interests require him to give her contraceptive advice, treatment or both without the parental consent.

A full discussion of the implications of Gillick competence and the Fraser Guidelines can be found in Daniels and Jenkins (2010).

COUNSELLING AND PSYCHOTHERAPY IN THE SAFEGUARDING CONTEXT

In working with young people the British Association for Counselling and Psychotherapy (BACP, 2013: 5) states:

Working with young people requires specific ethical awareness and competence. The practitioner is required to consider and assess the balance between young people's dependence on adults and carers and their progressive development towards acting independently. Working with children and young people requires careful consideration of issues concerning their capacity to give consent to receiving any service independently of someone with parental responsibilities and the management of confidences disclosed by clients.

They additionally state (BACP, 2010: 46) that: 'BACP believes that the physical safety of a young person is paramount and that young people in counselling will be led to understand that there are certain limits to confidentiality.'

The first statement by the BACP acknowledges some of the principles that underpin Gillick competence and Fraser Guidelines: that children and young people are in a process of psychological, emotional, physical and cognitive development that means that, at any given time, their capacity to understand the world around them is in a process of change. It is this challenge in working with children and young people, and vulnerable adults, that must sit at the heart of our work: that a client's capacity or competence to make decisions for themselves will always be a central factor when working with risk.

For many therapists, the response to risk with children and young people is clearly defined by local safeguarding procedures in which their work is framed. The difficult challenges come when we begin to determine the nature and extent of risk. For example, consider the following scenarios.

Responding to risk in therapy: Ed

Ed is 14 years old and is seeing a counsellor in a school setting. He feels quite low and has told his counsellor that sometimes he 'wants to go to sleep and not wake up'. His counsellor has asked Ed specific questions about his level of risk and Ed has said that he does not intend to act on these thoughts, they just represent how he feels sometimes; he would rather the school did not know about his feelings. The school's safeguarding policy states that any reference to suicide, no matter how vague or low-level, must be reported immediately to the school safeguarding lead.

Responding to risk in therapy: Lesley

Lesley is a 16-year-old seeing a counsellor in a Further Education setting. She has self-referred with issues of anger, together with family problems. During assessment Lesley tells her counsellor that she has self-injured for some years – cutting her stomach and arms. The safeguarding policy states that issues of self-harm should be flagged with the Safeguarding Coordinator, but Lesley's counsellor is reluctant to do so.

Responding to risk in therapy: Adam

Adam is 22 years old with moderate learning difficulties. He attends a supported adult placement daily and has been referred for counselling. During counselling he talks about one of the members of staff who 'touches' him sometimes in a way he finds confusing: sometimes he enjoys the feelings but feels uncomfortable that it is happening. He is frightened to tell anyone because he also likes the member of staff and doesn't want to get him into trouble.

Each of these scenarios represents different challenges and draw on the principles we have outlined throughout this chapter. Keeping the above situations in mind we might suggest the following indicators for good practice:

- Ensure you have a sense of the client's capacity or competence at any given point, evaluating their ability to understand the process of therapy and make decisions accordingly.
- Ensure that clients fully understand the limitations of confidentiality and what might happen in the event of having to break confidentiality (e.g. who you might need to speak to, and why).
- Ensure that you fully understand the limitations of confidentiality, how they relate to any policies or procedures in place in the setting, and how you would manage passing on concerns to another person (and who that person would be).
- Know what the policies and procedures around safeguarding are (children and young people, or vulnerable adults, depending on context) and how you would be expected to respond in any given situation involving risk.
- If a policy instructs you to act in a certain way, then do so. Failure to follow policy, even if you disagree with it, leaves both you and your client in a vulnerable position.
- If you disagree with any safeguarding policy, find appropriate mechanisms to ensure a discussion takes place where your concerns can be raised, wherever possible.
- If there are no policies in place in an organisation, trigger discussions with relevant personnel, if possible, to ascertain a shared understanding of practice.
- If there are no policies in place because you work as an independent practitioner, consider developing guidelines for yourself so that you can have a clear structure of thinking when necessary and provide an equitable and fair service.
- Ensure you have full discussions with your supervisor about the implications of safeguarding for your practice, and what your supervisor might additionally expect from you.
- Ensure you are fully aware of legal parameters that might inform areas of practice, and follow them carefully.
- Ensure you are fully aware of ethical guidance from professional organisations that might inform your practice, and follow that guidance carefully.
- Always record concerns fully and accurately – ensuring you keep to the facts and avoid conjecture or opinion.
- Always record actions taken in response to concerns, detailing: the nature and extent of the concern, the agreed response, the steps taken to reach the agreed response, the client's perspective, the outcome of the response. Additionally include a rationale for why a client's known wishes were disregarded, if they were.

- Make clear in your notes any evaluation of Gillick competence if working with children and young people, and/or mental capacity for people over 16, to provide a clear context for decisions made.
- If you have concerns about the immediate wellbeing of a child or young person, or a vulnerable adult, act.

While I appreciate that many of you will have wanted to read a definitive guide as to what to do and how to respond, it is simply not possible to provide this. The nature of counselling and psychotherapy means that we are always working with unique circumstances, even if there are common characteristics across client groups and presentations. Each situation demands a clear process of thought, always discussed with a line manager or supervisor, and enacted empathically and sensitively.

Chapter summary

In this chapter we have considered the concepts of safeguarding and child protection. We have located child protection as an aspect of safeguarding in which the safety of a child or young person up to the age of 18 will be assessed and acted on if they are deemed to be at risk of, or suffering from, abuse. However, we have outlined that safeguarding goes beyond the specific task of child protection and instead focuses on the wider wellbeing of the person, including the push for positive outcomes. Safeguarding principles can be applied to children and young people, but also to vulnerable adults. With respect to younger clients we have considered the implications of Gillick competence and the Fraser Guidelines, and with respect to vulnerable adults we have re-visited the concepts surrounding mental capacity. Finally, we have considered some important good practice indicators for therapists when working within the context of safeguarding.

8

MENTAL HEALTH CRISIS: DANGER AND OPPORTUNITY

Chapter outline

Mental health crisis is the subject of much research, yet counsellors and psychotherapists are generally poorly equipped by their training to respond to an individual in crisis; specific skills are required and these will be highlighted. The factors that might lead an individual into mental health crisis will be explored, and an overview given of primary diagnostic factors that might be relevant. How mental health 'systems' work will be highlighted. Finally, the concept of crisis as a time of opportunity as well as danger will be discussed.

INTRODUCTION

While we have considered very specific risk situations that might present in counselling and psychotherapy, such as risk of suicide, the risk of mental health crisis is also an important factor to consider. Such crisis may involve a risk of suicide or of harm to others, but not necessarily. It may be the client presents no physical risk to themselves or to other people, but a rapid deterioration in their mental health has left them in a highly confused and vulnerable state. Counsellors and psychotherapists in the UK are not diagnosticians; that is, they are not involved in conferring a mental health diagnosis on their client. Most typically, this would be undertaken by a GP, a psychiatrist or sometimes a clinical psychologist. Likewise, someone experiencing severe mental health distress would usually be responded to in the first instance through primary or secondary care mental health services. However, it is not uncommon for therapy to be offered in mental health settings (and this was the setting in which I practised for many years), or for people to be referred to counselling as part of their hospital discharge plan, or for more severe mental health problems to emerge during the process of therapy. As such, it is vital that therapists are aware of the key risks that might present with mental health crisis, the indicators that the client may be experiencing a mental health crisis, as well as the therapeutic opportunities that might be created as a consequence, assuming the safety and wellbeing of the client.

The extent to which therapists are equipped to work with severe mental health distress is uncertain. There is a full range of approaches in therapy training, from courses with extensive teaching input regarding diagnostic structures and psychopathology, including the requirement for a mental health placement, through to courses with no such input at all. Sometimes this is simply due to the quality of the teaching programme itself, while at other times it might reflect the philosophy of the therapeutic model being taught. For example, person-centred theory has traditionally rejected a medical model of mental health and has distanced itself from the concept of diagnostic structure (Sanders, 2007). Some writers, theorists and researchers have looked at bridging some of the theories of psychopathology with aspects of the person-centred approach, without diluting or compromising either, but essentially person-centred therapy remains a non-medicalising therapy (Joseph and Worsley, 2005; Sommerbeck, 2003). Psychodynamic practice has been more open to the idea of mental health diagnosis, making use of such ideas more proactively and positively, while cognitive behavioural approaches are more engaged again with ideas from psychiatry and mental health. This is a rather crude demarcation however, as practitioners who espouse different models will make use of such ideas to a greater or lesser extent.

My intention in this chapter is to provide a brief overview of how mental health services are generally structured and accessed in the UK, some key information about the types of mental health presentations that might develop into crisis, and the 'signs and symptoms' to look for, how to recognise whether someone is moving into a mental health crisis. Supervision is key to working with clients presenting with mental health problems, and particularly so if you have little or no experience in mental health settings.

THE NATURE OF MENTAL HEALTH DIAGNOSES

In thinking about the potential for mental health crisis and the risks that might arise as a consequence, it is helpful to briefly reflect on the nature of mental health diagnosis, which is usually drawn from diagnostic manuals such as *DSM-V* (American Psychiatric Association, 2013) and *ICD-10* (World Health Organization, 1992). The degree and extent to which an individual therapist will engage with the nature of mental health diagnosis will be dependent on a number of factors, including:

- The therapist's core training, how much that was diagnostically informed
- The working context of the therapist and the extent to which diagnostic ideas are actively used
- The therapist's own experience of mental health systems
- Personally held views about the nature of mental health distress
- Professional experience with previous clients
- Professional experience of other agencies, either currently or in the past.

This is relevant because it will shape how the therapist understands their client's experience and risk, and ways in which they can be supported, as well as how they might respond. The approach to mental health diagnosis is very similar to that of the diagnosis of physical health problems, which in itself attracts criticism on the grounds that some argue it is not appropriate to apply the same ideas of pathology to the mind as to the body (Ellerby, 2007; Newnes and Dunn, 1999). The sometimes ill-defined and abstract nature of mental health distress makes it impossible to accurately categorise in the same way as physical health problems, some argue.

In physical medicine the medic has available to them a number of tests to determine the existence of illness; this is not the case in mental health. Rather, such a diagnosis is made on the observation and evaluation of the mental health professional, which diagnostic structures aim to make as objective as possible. It might be argued however, that rather than mental health diagnosis being an objective evaluation using scientifically proven criteria, as it is claimed to be, it is rather a subjective interpretation of a number of factors and a best judgement based on available information. The accuracy or otherwise of this assertion would take many pages to unpack, but for the sake of this chapter it is an interesting assertion and one that is probably true for the counsellor or psychotherapist working with their client in most settings. Making sense of a client's mental health state is as likely to be as much about your experience of that person in relation to their usual presentation or, for new clients, a typical presentation. Risk then is experienced and evaluated in a context of interpretation.

MENTAL HEALTH SYSTEMS AND LEGISLATIVE FRAMEWORK

In thinking about responding to risk, it is helpful to have at least a general understanding of mental health support networks. The outline I offer is applicable to a UK setting, but is probably transferable to comparable systems. For the sake of accessibility I will outline four layers of mental health support: *third sector and social care*; *primary*; *secondary*; and *allied*.

Mental health systems: third sector and social care

While most people think of statutorily funded mental health systems when they think of mental health care, it is probably true that the majority of mental health support is delivered by third sector organisations in community settings, such as drop-in centres, home visiting and job creation schemes, as well as more specific therapeutic interventions in counselling and psychotherapy services. Such provision is structured across national, well-known organisations such as MIND and SANE, as well as many more smaller charitable organisations delivering small but important projects. As the 'threshold' for referral to statutory services has increased, meaning that more people do not meet referral criteria and yet remain vulnerable, third sector provision has become even more important. It is typified by dedicated people offering often life-saving interventions typically on a voluntary basis, or certainly low-paid; the importance of their support cannot be overstated. Social care services, again available through third sector organisations but also statutory social services, offer a great deal of support through the delivery of social work services, home and community support and advice.

Mental health systems: primary care

Primary care services refer mostly to GP practices located in community settings. This is often the first point of contact for most people experiencing mental health distress and might be the point at which an initial mental health diagnosis is made. Primary care services deliver care to the majority of people who access statutorily funded health services and often the GP and other related personnel, such as mental health nurses and primary care link staff, respond to the needs of people experiencing mental health distress. Additionally, some therapy services, typically provided through the Improving Access to the Psychological Therapies (IAPT) programme, are accessed through primary care for people with mild to moderate depression and anxiety, for example.

Primary care also offers a 'gateway' provision for people with more complex needs or those in crisis, having easy access to secondary care services for more specialist assessment or response. In many geographical locations a primary care network is the only mechanism for accessing secondary care services, with such services only accepting referrals from GPs. This is not necessarily true across the board however, and it is important you ascertain the systems of referral that apply in your setting. As such, it is vitally important that the therapy services have at least the name of a client's GP at the point of referral, in case there should be a necessity to respond to risk.

Mental health settings: secondary

Secondary care services are structured slightly differently across the country but typically offer mental health intervention to people with more complex mental health needs, or for those in crisis. Services are often structured across in-patient units (where people can be admitted to hospital for assessment and/or treatment), and out-patient services, where people can attend to be evaluated by their psychiatrist, clinical psychologist, mental health nurse or social worker, for example. A mental health diagnosis may be made, or reviewed, and treatment can be monitored and changed, and a range of therapeutic services can be delivered, again in some instances through the IAPT provision, for more complex needs and for those people who have not responded to primary early interventions.

In addition to in- and out-patient services, a range of other teams are located in secondary care services offering more specialist assessment and interventions, such as crisis response or home treatment teams, assertive outreach (where active steps are taken to engage 'hard to reach' people), early intervention psychosis teams (delivering quick services to young people with signs of psychosis), eating disorder services (offering specialised therapeutic and medical input for people with a diagnosed eating disorder), as well as services such as Child and Adolescent Mental Health Services (CAMHS), responding to the needs of children and young people. Such services are usually accessed either via primary care, such as the client's GP, or other secondary care services, such as one of the mental health professionals outlined above. Other than crisis intervention services, it is rare for secondary care services to be available for anyone to refer to, however, it is important that you are aware of the structure and nature of secondary care services in your locality so that, should you need to refer a client to their GP, you might additionally be able to outline the sort of services you would like them to consider, as well as explaining such services fully to your client.

Mental health services: allied

I include this category as there is a whole range of people offering important mental health support who do not easily fit into the above three categories. Most essential is the informal support that is offered, including family and friends. It is probably true that the entire mental health network would collapse without the tireless, unconditional support that comes in the shape of a telephone call received just at the right time, or a safe space to sleep, or some food on the table. Mental health problems are linked with poverty (Topor et al., 2013), and, I would assert, both resource and relational poverty. By resource poverty I mean the lack of appropriate supported accommodation, food, money and the very basic needs that Maslow (1943) outlined many years ago. By relational poverty I mean the lack of human contact, unconditional love and care, and a listening ear that can quickly transform someone's world from a lonely, dark and isolated space into something more meaningful.

Beyond this is a swathe of other workers, in housing, health, social and other networks, who offer interventions that support mental health needs. I would include a large number of counsellors and psychotherapists, positioned outside of the health, social and third party sectors, whose delivery of mental health support (even if they don't always describe it as that) is vital. Therapy services can be found in education (schools, further and higher education settings), the community and the independent sector, for example, and can often help people avoid referral to secondary care services and thus have an important diverting role.

Legislative overview

The Mental Capacity Act (2005) enshrines in law the concept that all adults (including 16–18-year-olds) have capacity unless there is evidence for them having temporarily lost capacity due to illness or distress. This is specifically stated in the Act as:

- Can the client understand the information needed to make the decision?
- Can the client remember that information for long enough to make the decision?
- Can the client weigh up the consequences of deciding one way or another?
- Can the client communicate their decision?

We have the right under law to make decisions that affect our lives, including refusal of treatment and deciding to end our lives (this is different from assisted suicide), even if those decisions are considered to be unwise. While other factors will influence the decisions made in counselling and psychotherapy, such as the contract and the context of therapy, including policies and procedures informing the work, mental capacity remains an important legal imperative for all in practice.

In terms of mental health law, the Mental Health Act (1983, amended in 2007) informs all decisions made about the compulsory detention and treatment of individuals suffering from mental health distress – or mental 'illness' as the Act terms it. There are set procedures that must be followed if a person is to be compulsorily detained in hospital or treated against their will. There must be medical recommendations for treatment, and an Approved Mental Health Professional (AMHP) can only make an application based on those recommendations. The Act allows for the compulsory admission to hospital under the following terms:

- *Section 2*: where a person can be admitted to hospital for up to 28 days for assessment
- *Section 3*: where a person can be admitted to hospital for up to 6 months for assessment and treatment
- *Section 4*: where a person can be admitted to hospital for up to 72 hours for assessment only, based on one (rather than two) medical recommendations (an emergency admission)
- *Section 134*: where a person can be admitted to hospital for assessment for 72 hours from a private residence that the authorities can enter by force, but only with a magistrate's warrant
- *Section 136*: where the police can detain someone to a place of safety (often an Accident and Emergency Department) for up to 72 hours for assessment. Both with s134 and s136, the person must either be discharged or the section converted to a s2 or s3 at the end of the 72-hour period.

This is helpful information for therapists to be aware of in terms of the legality of detention. However, therapists would not qualify as an AMHP and, as such, would never be in the position to determine whether compulsory hospitalisation is required. The first contact for this process would typically be the client's GP or a mental health crisis team.

Overall, it is essential that counsellors and psychotherapists take time and care in ensuring they are fully aware of what services exist in their area, the scope and nature of services, how they can be accessed, including referral routes, and have this information and knowledge to hand before such information is needed. When supporting people either moving into crisis or already in crisis, a fundamental skill is the capacity to contain chaos and offer the client a grounded space in which they can feel safe and held. While there are therapeutic skills for achieving this, the provision of timely and accurate information is a fundamental aspect of that process that should not be underestimated. If when talking to a client about the possibility of a referral on to a crisis team the client asks, 'Who are they and what will they do?', the client needs to hear a solid answer as a response of 'I don't know' is more likely to aggravate their concerns than reduce them.

PRESENTING PROBLEMS AND WORKING WITH RISK

It is impossible in the space available to provide an in-depth consideration of all mental health problems, how they might present and how best to respond to them. The truth is that when people begin to move into a state of crisis, there are few therapists – usually because of insufficient training, or the context of their therapy provision – who can provide the level of intervention required to help keep people safe. That is not to say that therapy is not important in such situations, or cannot contribute to the client's recovery, because it has an absolutely pivotal role in these respects. However, during a period of crisis people will often need a level of containment and safety that cannot be delivered in a 50-minute therapy session.

The primary task, therefore, is for the therapist to be able to detect when a person might be moving into crisis and consider, in collaboration with the client, the most appropriate response. Sometimes that will be to work proactively with the client to help them feel safe while continuing with the therapy (usually if the crisis has been picked up early enough), or for a referral on to more specialist assessment with the option of continuing with therapy once the crisis has passed. The concept of the mental state examination can be helpful here in providing a structure within which the therapist can begin to evaluate different aspects of their client's presentation. Russello (2008: 4) offers a useful overview of key aspects of a mental state examination:

> The aim is to assess the state of mind at the time the interview is being conducted. Information about each of the headings is observed or elicited by the therapist or volunteered by the client:
>
> - Appearance and behaviour: what is the client's general appearance, eye contact, self-care, facial expression, posture, motor activity, movements?
> - Speech: how are they speaking, what is the content, rate, quantity, pattern and continuity of ideas?
> - Thought: what is the content? Are there preoccupations, obsessions, overvalued ideas, delusions, suicidal thoughts?
> - Mood: (subjective, as expressed by client) what is the prevailing mood? Are there variations or incongruence, i.e., are they saying they are sad while smiling happily?
> - Affect: observed, external manifestations of emotion, e.g., are they frowning or smiling?
> - Abnormal experiences: does the client relate any sense of depersonalisation (client feels unreal) and derealisation (experiences others as lifeless)?
> - Beliefs: delusions (false beliefs held with absolute conviction and not amenable to argument or to explanation in terms of the individual's culture)
> - Perception: does the client describe or seem to have any hallucinations (a false perception arising without an external stimulus)?
> - Cognition: how is client's orientation (of time, place and person), attention (ability to focus on a specific issue), concentration (ability to sustain the focus), memory (short/long term)?
> - Insight: how much awareness do they have about what they are presenting? Do they believe themselves ill and in need of treatment, and to what do they attribute their symptoms?

The implication here is clear that the sooner we can identify the potential for an emerging crisis the more able we are to work with the level of risk. In this sense working with risk in mental health crisis is the same as in any presenting situation: the sooner we can identify with the client a potential risk and work proactively with it, the better chance we both have in mitigating the potential for a harmful outcome. The later this identification takes place the more likely the level of risk will increase to a point where it is no longer containable or workable with in the therapeutic frame.

It is not my intention here to offer detailed analysis of the diagnostic criteria for each presentation discussed. For that I would recommend other resources (such as: American Psychiatric Association, 2013; Lemma, 1996; World Health Organization, 1992). Instead, my intention is to offer a brief description of how the problem might present and how clients might begin to present with risk. We will try to identify key 'red flag' points, where the therapist needs to be mindful of whether the risk is still safely containable within the therapeutic frame in relation to three mental health presentations that can present particular challenges in practice.

Presenting problems and working with risk: depression

Depression is a term that has fallen into daily parlance and is used to describe a range of feelings from feeling generally low, through to debilitating and crushing flatness and disconnection. As such, the danger for us as practitioners is that we become immune to the potential dangers of depression and potentially miss the risks that might be associated with it. Gilbert (2007: 5) offers a definition of depression across four main areas:

- *Motivation*: apathy, loss of energy and interest, things seem pointless, hopeless
- *Emotional*: depressed mood, plus emptiness, anger or resentment, anxiety, shame and guilt
- *Cognitive*: poor concentration, negative ideas about the self, the world and the future
- *Biological*: sleep disturbance, loss of appetite, changes in sleep and levels of libido, and changes in hormones and brain chemicals.

While not all approaches to therapy would include the concept of a formal assessment in their work, the therapist's evaluation of these issues, in collaboration with their clients, can not only provide important therapeutic insights and opportunities for change but also help keep both therapist and client open to the dangers and risks that might also present. As with some other mental health presentations, risk is likely to arise according to the severity of the presenting problems, and their potential for harm cannot be underestimated. Some risks associated with depression include:

- Risk of suicide, specifically related to hopelessness
- Risk of suicide, particularly when depression begins to lift slightly and the client has more energy and wherewithal to act on their thoughts

- Risk of neglect, through not eating, sleeping or neglecting more general self-care
- Risk of physical and psychological withdrawal, where clients disconnect from those around them and their world
- Risk of the emergence of other mental health problems, such as anxiety or psychosis.

It is important to keep in mind that a client's physical presentation can tell us as much as what they describe. A client who presents with a lack of self-care, or where there is deterioration in the level of self-care over time, is someone who needs careful attention and an open discussion about their safety and wellbeing. Some pointers for good practice in relation to depression and risk include (Reeves, 2013b: 201):

- Undertaking an assessment or evaluation of your client's mental health
- Encouraging your client to make contact, or maintain contact with the GP for regular review
- Taking a holistic approach to working with depression, remembering that social and physical factors are as relevant and important to the client and the nature of risk as psychological ones
- Ensuring that sessions are scheduled for when the client is best able to make use of them (for example, early morning sessions might be difficult for a client with disrupted sleep patterns)
- Ensuring regular reviews so that you can collaboratively monitor progress or change (both for the better and worse)
- Helping the client to understand the nature of their fluctuating mood so that they can monitor changes and pick up on them quickly too
- Paying careful attention to the risk of suicide, or the presence of self-injury and self-harm, in reflecting on your client's safety.

Presenting problems and working with risk: psychosis

The Royal College of Psychiatrists (2010) outline a number of key symptoms of psychosis:

- The client hears, feels, smells or sees things that other people do not (*hallucinations*)
- The client may have strange thoughts or beliefs that may make the person feel they are being controlled, persecuted or harassed (*delusions*). It is important to consider thoughts or beliefs in the context of cultural appropriateness for the client
- The client may have muddled or blocked thinking (*thought disorder*)
- The client may, at times, seem unusually excited or withdrawn and avoid contact with people (*isolation or agitation*)
- The client will often fail to realise there is anything wrong with them (*lack of insight*).

Not all of these symptoms need to be present to define psychosis, and some may fluctuate over time or deteriorate quite quickly. The evaluation of psychosis is complex and takes place over time, given there is no single test to determine the presence of a psychotic process. The key message here is that if any one of the symptoms outlined above are apparent in a therapy session, and cannot be explained by another cause, such as alcohol or drug use, then the therapist should be alert to the possibility of referral to the client's GP for further assessment. The sooner this can take place the better for the client, as research suggests that early intervention in psychosis can be effective in establishing efficacious treatment plans and preventing further deterioration or the development of other mental health problems.

Psychosis can develop at any age, but young people are particularly vulnerable to what is described as 'early onset' psychosis. However, psychosis can also be triggered by other actions, such as the use of drugs or alcohol (drug-induced psychosis), for example. If diagnosis is suspected then the therapist should express concern about the client's wellbeing (without necessarily using the term 'psychosis', as we are not diagnosticians), and arrange for early referral for assessment and treatment. This does not preclude the continuation of therapy, as this can often be very helpful, but therapy usually takes place in conjunction with other approaches rather than on its own. Keeping in mind the client's mental capacity here is important as, with the lack of insight often associated with psychosis, the client may be unwilling to consider a GP referral given they may not consider anything to be wrong. Sometimes the therapist will need to act without the consent of the client if they believe the client's mental health is deteriorating and the client has temporarily lost mental capacity, as can sometimes be the case with psychosis.

Presenting problems and working with risk: eating disorders

Eating disorders are possibly the most difficult to work with in terms of risk given their potential lethality, but propensity to be hidden by the client. It is very possible for a very underweight person to mask their body shape, size and weight through carefully selected clothing. There are a number of types of eating disorders, but two most commonly seen in therapy are bulimia nervosa (binge eating and the management of weight and body size through purging or non-purging type behaviours) and anorexia nervosa (weight reduction through fasting). Both have potential lethality, through weight loss but also dangerous biochemical changes that can be triggered through a disordered diet and vomiting.

It is important that therapists feel confident in being able to talk openly to clients about eating disorders, and ask about eating patterns in the early stages of therapy. The NICE guidelines for the treatment of eating disorders identify the following areas for assessment (NICE, 2004: 36):

- Current and past physical health and treatment
- Cognitive abilities
- Any present physical disabilities
- A historical and current assessment of family and interpersonal relationships
- Mental state and personality factors
- Social circumstances and support
- Occupational and social functioning
- Educational and vocational needs.

I would also add (Reeves, 2013b: 211):

- Understanding of the therapeutic process and willingness to engage
- Willingness for the appropriate and informed liaison between you and others involved in providing care (e.g. GP)
- Preferably a recent health check by the client's GP and plans for ongoing monitoring of the client's physical health needs
- Clearly defined and agreed boundaries of confidentiality should you have concerns (based on whatever information is available to you) should your client's health deteriorate or weight drop, *even if you only suspect that is the case*
- An agreement between you and your client about the focus of the therapy (which might not ultimately be about their relationship with food).

Some therapists will feel more competent and able to address some of these areas than others. What is important is that you work confidently using your own experience and capacity, and gather what information you consider pertinent to help determine, with your client, their capacity to work effectively and safely in therapy. The additional parameters I have added around therapy specifically are helpful in setting out the basis for any work. To respond effectively to apparent risk it is essential that an honest dialogue is established from the beginning and that the client is willing and able to work with that. Ultimately, therapists need to give themselves permission to act on concerns, even when they are only suspected, given that often there will be a lack of 'proof' of weight loss or other deterioration.

Presenting problems and working with risk: 'grounding' techniques

When seeing someone in crisis it is not uncommon for them to be in a highly agitated state. Typically there is very little that can be proactively done until the client is safely contained and psychologically 'grounded'. A few simple techniques, if delivered with confidence, authority and empathy, can be highly effective in helping the client feel grounded so that other discussions can take place. Such skills include the following.

Immediate techniques

- Breathing exercises: calm breathing counting to three on each in/out breath.
- A 'rescue breath': where the client is encouraged to take **one** deep breath in, as deeply as possible, and then blow the breath out as hard as possible. This can help relax the diaphragm and begin to regulate agitated breathing. Only do this once or twice as the client can begin to hyperventilate otherwise.
- Positive self-talk: *I am going to be all right; nothing awful is going to happen to me; I can cope with this situation.*
- Contact: encouraging clients either to make eye contact with you or to look at something static and physical in the room to help them connect back with their surroundings.
- Voice: another mechanism for helping the client to reconnect if in a highly agitated place; talking to the client calmly but confidently, and asking the client to focus on your voice.
- Physical grounding: to encourage the client to sit down and feel the chair supporting them – to use the chair as a wider metaphor for support and safety.

Ongoing techniques

- Guided imagery: to help the client focus on inner, healing and calm thoughts and to create a safe place they can go to at times of difficulty or crisis.
- Self-help resources: such as books, CDs and relaxation videos on social media sites, that you have previously viewed and can recommend with confidence.
- Avoiding stimulants: such as caffeine, alcohol and drugs (beyond those prescribed by a medical practitioner).
- Developing meditation techniques: including introducing clients to mindfulness approaches.
- Other support: including speaking with a GP or trusted friend, for example.

Mental health crisis can bring many risks, including those of suicide and self-injury, but other risks too, including dissociation, self-neglect, withdrawal from family, friends and society and psychosis, for example. The above techniques can be useful in helping the client manage crisis when it occurs, but further support may be indicated.

Chapter summary

In this chapter we have considered what is meant by mental health crisis, and how it can bring with it a range of risk scenarios that can leave the client in a vulnerable place. In considering this we have taken a critical view of mental health systems and considered some of the criticisms made. We have looked at how services are generally structured in the UK and the legal parameters that can inform practice. In looking at a few 'red flag' conditions that can be particularly problematic in therapy, we have outlined a number of good practice indicators and techniques for supporting clients.

9

USING SUPERVISION TO MANAGE RISKS IN THE THERAPEUTIC PROCESS

Chapter outline

In this chapter we will consider a number of specific risks that can arise in the therapeutic process, such as crossing boundaries (sexual, financial), exploitation of clients, lack of ethical thinking, as well as risks to the therapist, such as poor self-care, burnout and vicarious trauma. We will then consider ways in which we might support ourselves in working with these risks, such as in supervision.

INTRODUCTION

Throughout the previous chapters we have considered particular situational risks as presented by clients, such as suicide risk, risks associated with self-harm and self-injury, as well as violence to others and safeguarding concerns. This is how we often think about working with risk: a situation arises that is related to a client's distress that we have to evaluate and respond to. Perhaps we are focused on working with these particular risks because they are sufficiently discrete and obvious that they have the potential to cause anxiety if we 'get things wrong' in how we respond. As a straw poll I talked with a number of therapists about the fact that I was writing a book about working with risk in counselling and psychotherapy and asked them what they considered to be the most pertinent issues to consider. Without fail they all responded with the risk of suicide and self-harm and the fear of 'getting it wrong'.

However, while these issues are indeed important, my view is that we would limit our thinking by focusing only on the situational risks, and need instead to widen our thinking about working with risk to incorporate a number of others that can also have the potential for negative outcome. As we have discussed previously, there are all sorts of risks inherent in the therapeutic process that need attention and care, as well as the therapeutic opportunities that can sometimes be afforded if these risks are managed with consideration.

The purpose of this chapter therefore, is to think about the range of risks that we might encounter in our work as counsellors and psychotherapists, and how they might present quite obviously, but at other times be more embedded in a process and thus more easily missed. The role of supervision is integral here in providing us with an important resource in our work to step back from the moment-by-moment experience of therapy and take a wider view of what might be taking place.

THINKING ABOUT RISKS IN THERAPY

While risk can be defined in all sorts of different ways depending on the context in which it is being viewed (health risk, financial risk, emotional risk, etc.), I suggested in Chapter 2 five parameters for thinking about risk in terms of counselling and psychotherapy: situational; relational; contextual; professional; and personal. The situational risks are those that most easily come to mind, including risk of suicide and self-harm. Depending on the setting, other situational risks might be at the forefront of thinking too, such as where there are safeguarding concerns of the risk of violence to others. I hope to offer below a brief commentary on the types of risks that might present within the other parameters and then consider ways in which we might engage in a proactive response.

Relational risks

Relational risks primarily describe those situations that emerge from and sit within the relational process. Like all relationships, the therapeutic relationship is a mixture of the spoken and unspoken, the done and the not done, the felt and the avoided, thought and distraction. It is a complex interplay between two people (in individual therapy), or several people (in group therapy), that either takes place face to face or virtually, perhaps online or on the telephone, for example. Arguably all therapeutic modalities are dependent on the successful establishment of a therapeutic alliance, and many therapeutic approaches will explicitly make use of the process of the relationship as part of the nature of change. Relational risks are those that sit within that complex interplay that might be apparent, or might emerge slowly over time. Such risks include:

The 'corruption of friendship'

Masson talks about the corruption of friendship. His writing explores the difficult boundaries between the intimacy of therapy and how that builds on a notion of friendship that isn't actually in place. Masson (1988: 30) states that:

> The client is offered a relationship that may appear to be a friendship, in that he or she is encouraged to share his or her closest secrets and feelings, but that is in reality a false friendship. The relationship between therapist and client ... is a professional one based on an inequality of power.

The risk here is of the client being deliberately, or accidentally, misled as to the nature and form of the therapeutic relationship. The imperative is for the therapist to talk openly about how therapy works so that the client is able to make an informed decision about entering into it. Boundaries need not only to be clear but also clearly articulated in a way the client can understand and make their own sense of. It is an ethical duty to ensure that the client is clear and that you, as therapist, are sure the client is clear.

Sexual attraction

The therapeutic relationship is often a very intimate one. As outlined in the previous section, clients are provided with space and opportunity to discuss and explore the most vulnerable parts of themselves in collaboration with a therapist who, regardless of orientation, is likely to offer warmth, empathy and understanding. It is not uncommon for such feelings of warmth and care to be confusing and difficult for the client to accept, perhaps for the first time in their lives. A client's experience of sexual attraction to the therapist is understandable in this context and needs to be recognised and worked with positively and supportively so that the client does not experience shame or harsh rejection. Holding the clear boundary that separates the therapeutic relationship from other forms of relationship needs to be affirmed implicitly and, where needed, explicitly, throughout the process. It is also not rare for therapists to experience sexual attraction towards their clients. Neither of these scenarios should come as a surprise or a shock: regardless of the role of 'client' or 'counsellor', the process is ultimately two or more people meeting in an intimate exchange. The client's vulnerability because of the dynamics of trust, sharing, distress, openness and power, for example, are the reasons why such boundaries need to be held carefully and respected at all times, even when the actual therapy is over.

Cultural dominance

In this sense 'culture' is meant with a capital 'C' – those aspects of self that are defined by beliefs, ideas, faith, language and behaviour most commonly associated with ethnicity – and also a small 'c' – those aspects of self that are defined and shaped by supplementary identities, such as groups, gangs or art, for example. The idea of culture here is a broadly drawn one that incorporates a full range of characteristics and qualities at the heart of an individual's experience and identity. Problems can emerge when difference is not acknowledged and we take an 'everyone is the same' position. The risk of cultural dominance is of the therapist, deliberately or accidentally, presenting a dominant view of the client's problem informed by his or her own cultural position. The power imbalance in therapy can allow for such dominance to be internalised by the client, with a potential sense of loss of 'self', or shame deriving from a position previously held that no longer seems acceptable.

The exploitation of power

Following on from the ideas of cultural dominance is the exploitation of power – that is, the therapist using their personal and institutional power to create a therapeutic direction for a client because they believe it is right (in their experience) and which does not involve the client in a collaborative exploration of their presenting issues. This is most likely to happen in those relationships where the therapist is unwilling or unable to recognise the power they might possess in the relationship. This is commonly the case for those modalities that privilege the expertise of the client. It can feel personally uncomfortable as a therapist to acknowledge personal power when philosophically we would prefer to locate it in the client. That is not to say the client is ultimately powerless, but that the institutional 'roles' of client and therapist are not created equally, particularly in the first stages of therapy when the client is less likely to feel able to exert their own authority in the process.

Of course, and with respect to all points made in this section, the dynamic might be from client to counsellor as much as counsellor to client. The challenge is for the therapist to recognise the existence of such risks so they can work proactively with them.

Contextual risks

The context of counselling and psychotherapy is always an important influencing factor on the nature of the therapeutic process. It is arguably impossible to separate out the therapeutic relationship from the context in which it sits, whether it be a health care setting, school, further or higher education, third sector provider or independent practice, for example. Each setting will positively provide for the potential for successful outcome of therapy, but each also has the potential to hinder or introduce risks to that process also. It is important for therapists to carefully reflect on the nature of their work and how the contextual risks can either be managed, or at least mitigated. Such risks include:

Ambiguous contracting or absence of a contract

It has perhaps become a mantra throughout this book that the importance of clearly agreed boundaries outlined in a written working agreement or contract cannot be overstated. Many of the risks that occur in therapy, and their consequent harms, typically come from misunderstandings or misapprehensions about the nature of therapy. Whether it is how to respond to a client who is suicidal, how to deal with a suspected situation of child abuse, or how to work with a relational rupture following a misuse of power, all can be more clearly responded to within the agreed contract. The reverse is then obviously true: the absence of a contract, or a poorly drawn-up one, or one that is verbal only with no clear record kept of it creates the perfect environment for potential risks to become actual harmful outcomes.

Lack of equity in service provision

Lack of equity in service provision can present very real issues when clients do not know what to expect in any situation. This is similar to a poorly drawn-up contract, but is encountered usually at a more institutional level. One example would be an institution with a policy regarding how to respond to suicide potential in clients. I am aware of some policies that state that each individual therapist within the same organisation must determine how best to respond to suicidal thoughts.

As a client, therefore, I might be able to explore my suicidal thoughts with therapist A openly and honestly with my confidentiality respected, but should I be allocated to therapist B, who perhaps is less willing to work with suicide potential, I might find the same discourse leading to my confidentiality being compromised and mental health services being alerted to my risk. I might therefore wonder why therapists A and B should respond so differently to the same situation, the answer being: because the policy allowed them to. As a client I should have confidence in the consistency of the application of policy and procedure – that is, that it would be applied fairly and equitably to all clients, all of the time.

Incompatibility with the underpinning ethos of counselling and psychotherapy

Some institutional policies are risk averse in that they try to avoid any engagement with risk so as to protect the institution. I am aware of therapy agencies with policies that state that all therapy will be withdrawn from clients who are actively self-harming and that all self-harm should stop before therapy commences. The literature is fairly clear that self-harm is often about coping with intolerable distress and that, while it is self-destructive, it is sometimes inevitable until the client can be supported to: (a) explore their intolerable distress; and (b) find alternative and less destructive ways of managing feelings. It might be argued, therefore, that the withdrawal of therapy at a policy level is incompatible with the underpinning ethos of counselling and psychotherapy, which is about supporting distressed people to engage with the process of change and the development of effective and self-respectful coping strategies. This is one example, and the implications of such incompatibility can be found in other situations.

Contradictory, over-written or insufficient policy and procedure

Linked with policies and procedures that might be incompatible with the ethos of therapy are those policies and procedures that are so complex, incoherent or fraught with contradiction they become impossible to implement without introducing risk into the equation. Some of the policies or procedural documents on working with suicide fall into this difficulty, where if A happens then B, and if B happens then C, but if B doesn't happen then the counsellor might instead consider D, E, F or even G, and so on. Policies and procedures can be profoundly helpful in containing and informing some of the more difficult and challenging aspects of therapy, but cannot easily pin down the specifics of each eventuality, given the uncertainties of human behaviour.

Professional risks

Professional risks include difficulties in direct client contact as well as the implications of our actions in a wider role. The work of a counsellor or psychotherapist extends beyond the direct work with clients, as the process of counselling and psychotherapy extends beyond the 50-minute hour. The face-to-face contact (or online contact) represents only part of our relationship with a client, albeit a central one. How we communicate from the outset, through written information or web-based information, through to the management of the contract, missed or re-arranged sessions, note-taking, ending and the management of the confidential nature of the relationship that extends well beyond the final session, all require commensurate consideration so that the potential risks to the client, the process or to ourselves are acknowledged and managed. Such risks include the following.

Miscommunication of services

A client's first contact with therapy services is typically through written or online media, such as posters, advertisements or websites, for example. In this context the risks I am referring to are not necessarily related to blatantly misleading advertising, or making claims that are impossible to justify, as these would potentially be illegal or certainly unethical, but rather where the nuance of the detail of the therapy on offer does not quite reflect the client's experience. An example of this would be where it only becomes clear to the client that the therapy on offer is time-limited during therapy, while the therapist had assumed this was apparent. For the client the conscious or unconscious pacing of work (i.e. making decisions about when to talk about difficult material) then needs to change quickly and is outside of the client's control. Clearly there may be circumstances when this would be difficult to avoid, such as therapist ill-health but, wherever possible, it is our duty to ensure that the client not only understands what therapy is before they commence but also all the details that pertain to therapy that will shape and inform the nature of the alliance.

Ruptures in communications

In some ways ruptures in communications during the therapeutic process are unavoidable and, if managed carefully and sensitively, can make a positive contribution to trust and the depth of the relationship. The sorts of ruptures that can introduce risk into the process can be multi-fold, but might include failure to manage written or online communications effectively, misunderstandings, or simply paying insufficient attention to the tone of what is being written. Email is perhaps a particular issue here: it can be very easy to quickly send off an email without paying full attention to how it might be received by your client. These sorts of ruptures might not necessarily explicitly find their way into the relationship, if clients feel hurt and reluctant to talk about them, but have the potential to seriously undermine the depth of trust that client feels able to invest in the relationship.

Uncertain or inappropriately flexible boundaries

Most therapists would acknowledge the importance of the therapeutic frame (Gray, 1994) in containing the relationship. An array of changing boundaries might be included here when considering risk, such as therapy vs friendship, room, location, therapeutic space, or time. Taking the latter point, I have myself experienced a very well-meaning therapist extending time boundaries of a session as a response to my own vulnerability. His intention was, no doubt, to offer me support and time to explore my issues but was instead experienced by me as a change in the boundaries of time I had trusted were in place but then made future sessions more precarious because I was not sure when the session would end. This sort of inconsistency might be described by some as a micro rupture with little apparent consequence for risk; the danger, however, is that suddenly the explicit frame has changed for the client and potentially nothing is safe any longer. Micro ruptures can quickly lead to major risks to the efficacy and value of therapy.

Beyond therapy

All of these considerations have been explored in the context of ongoing therapy. It is important to remind ourselves of the importance of maintaining and respecting the therapeutic contract after the end of the therapy itself. It is always important to discuss explicitly with clients as part of the ending process how such issues will be managed once the face-to-face, or online, process has finished. Clients will not necessarily know or assume that the same level of care will be afforded them once they have stopped attending. Again, knowing this clearly can help the client continue to trust the value of the therapeutic relationship and might provide a safer environment for them to return to it later, if needed.

Personal risks

Our 'self' as therapist is the tool with which we work. While we might bring techniques, ideas and an array of interventions to the therapeutic table, the essence of our work is dependent on the foundation of the alliance. If we are absent from the process, no matter how skilled an actor we are, our clients will quickly detect incongruity and the relationship will flounder. In its most benign form that might mean that the client does not really take away from therapy what they might have done in different circumstances. The greater risk is that the client is harmed by this incongruity and that the therapist is also left diminished or damaged. Such risks include the following.

Pushing on regardless

We will often take great care and time in exploring with clients how they take care of themselves and how to be respectful of their needs, particularly at vulnerable times. It is not uncommon for us to have this important discussion with clients while feeling physically, emotionally and spiritually depleted ourselves. One can only imagine the scene: a client sits attentively while their therapist talks of the importance of self-care and only doing what we are able to do, while the therapists coughs, sneezes, wheezes and moans through the discourse. One might predict what would go through a client's mind during this effective display in incongruity and hypocrisy. While I am not advocating a position that does not take the client's needs into account when reflecting on our own capacity to work effectively, I am advocating the importance of self-care and self-respect for our own physical, emotional and mental health. If we cannot role model that for our clients then the risk is that the wider value of the work also becomes undermined.

Vicarious trauma and burnout

Vicarious trauma can be defined as a:

> transformation in the helper's inner sense of identity and existence that results from utilising controlled empathy when listening to clients' trauma-content narratives. In other words, Vicarious Trauma is what happens to your neurological (or cognitive), physical, psychological, emotional and spiritual health when you listen to traumatic stories day after day or respond to traumatic situations while having to control your reaction. (Vicarious Trauma Institute, 2014)

The latter part of this definition has particular resonance for therapists – 'controlled empathy when listening to clients' trauma-content narratives' – for this is something we find ourselves doing regularly. The personal risk of not paying attention to the potential for vicarious trauma, perhaps thinking that it wouldn't happen to us, is burnout. The four stages of burnout can be outlined as:

- *Physical, mental and emotional exhaustion* – where we feel that it is hard to hear anything more
- *Shame and doubt* – where we feel enormous guilt and shame for not being able to be as present with our clients any more
- *Cynicism and callousness* – where we begin to blame our clients for our own distress, or objectify them so they cease to become people, but rather objects of attack
- *Failure, helplessness and crisis* – where we cease to be able to function in any meaningful way in most or all aspects of our personal and professional lives.

I have known too many colleagues and friends who have struggled with this dynamic, and can also relate to certain points in my own career when I too can identify being caught in this process. None of us is immune and the risk is a very present one.

Incongruity

By incongruity I am referring to a difficult to pinpoint mismatch between personal and professional self. It is almost as if the professional self is a veneer that is bonded to the personal self but that is also beginning to detach. Congruity for me as a therapist is being able to be with clients as I am, while at the same time working within a clear professional frame: the 'professional' is what is defined and contained by the nature of our work rather than acting out a role. My own experience is that, no matter how distressed or vulnerable clients may be, they quickly identify personal/professional incongruity in their therapist and, as a consequence, take an emotional step back to protect themselves from uncertainty. In short, they sense that what they see is not necessarily what they get and this introduces important risks into the relationship.

Callousness and attack

Finally I would like to spend a little more time looking at the idea of callousness in the therapeutic relationship, as outlined in the section on vicarious trauma and burnout above. Therapy is like any context where large numbers of people who have particular needs of another are seen, such as Accident and Emergency Departments, primary care, or airports and railway stations, for example. At an institutional level it is very easy for people to be translated into commodities or objects to be processed, rather than seen as individuals. I have witnessed therapy organisations slipping into this many times over the years. When it happens at an institutional level it can easily be acted out at the individual level, with individual therapists beginning to see their clients as intrusions.

Typified by the response 'you think you've got problems' in the face of a client narrative, it is a position that lacks empathy and compassion and is a risk for all of us.

STRATEGIES FOR WORKING WITH RISK

Having identified a number of risks that might present during the course of therapy, it is important to consider ways in which we might respond to these. As stated throughout, while risks are usually associated with the potential for negative or harmful outcomes, they also provide important therapeutic opportunities where change can take place and insight be achieved that might not otherwise have been possible. I will explore a number of strategies here and take each one in turn, spending more time on supervision given its integral place in all our day-to-day work.

- Supervision
- Therapeutic transparency
- Professional action
- Strategies for self-care.

Supervision

The aim in this chapter is to outline a number of possible risk scenarios and how these might present in therapy, while at the same time raising a number of questions that hopefully will be of help in structuring our thinking about how best to respond to them. As a broad statement, the value of supervision is important to note here. In the UK supervision remains an ethical requirement of all therapists, and for important reasons. I have previously drawn together a number of key definitions of supervision (Carroll, 1996; Hess, 1980; Inskipp and Proctor, 2001) and summarised how these definitions outline key functions (Reeves, 2013b: 381–2). That supervision is:

- A relationship and a process
- A professional, formal working alliance
- A place where work with clients can be explored and discussed
- A relationship in which feedback can be given and received
- A space for personal and professional development and the development of efficacy as a 'helper'
- A time during which professional standards, ethics and care can be scrutinised.

I will briefly consider how each of these key aspects of supervision can be pivotal in providing a space where risks can be reflected on and explored, before moving on to looking at the risks themselves.

A relationship and a process

In this chapter we are reflecting on those risks that present during a process of therapy as opposed to those that are just related to a situation the client finds themselves in. One of the strengths of supervision is that it is a relationship that is centred around the process of therapy and then, in turn, on the process of supervision. What happens in therapy can be presented by the supervisee and discussed with the supervisor, but the context for this is the relationship between the supervisee and supervisor and how aspects of the therapy relationship might be paralleled in the supervisory one (Mattinson, 1975). For example, consider the brief scenario below.

Alice, Michael and Sandra

Alice is a 34-year-old client who is seeing her counsellor, Michael, due to low self-esteem and social anxiety. She is fearful of social situations and does not feel confident enough to manage them. This is causing problems in her life. Her partner is quite domineering and Alice has talked about the way she feels 'lost' and 'voiceless' in her relationship. The therapeutic relationship is a good one, but Alice regularly defers to Michael's 'expertise' and his powerful position as therapist. She is rarely able to assert herself in therapy, or in life. Michael presents his work with Alice to his supervisor, Sandra. He is tentative and uncertain and at the end asks Sandra what she thinks would be the best thing for him to do.

It seems that Michael is paralleling the process of therapy in supervision: Alice is tentative and defers to the authority of Michael, while Michael has then become tentative and defers to the authority of Sandra. This dynamic presents enormous opportunity for insight into the process Michael is going through (assuming the supervisor notices it and is able to reflect it back to him) which, in turn (and more importantly), provides an important opportunity to consider the situation Alice finds herself in. It provides a space for Michael to think in more depth about the nature of the relationship with Alice and how there may be two particular risks for him to be aware of: first, that he loses his own 'self' in the relationship by trying not to be like her domineering partner, just in the same way Alice has; or, second, that he over-compensates and becomes the domineering therapist. Either way, Alice does not get the space she needs because she remains silenced either by benign therapy or overwhelming therapy. This is also a good illustrative example of the point made throughout this book that while risks can be seen as dangers to the relationship (or client or therapist), they also provide important opportunities for insight and change.

A professional, formal working alliance

While supervision is a relationship and a process, it is one defined by particular tasks and is held, just like therapy, in the context of clear agreements for working and a contract that supports that. As such, one task of the supervisor in the early stages of supervision is to explore the supervisee's needs and goals in supervision and agree the parameters within which that might take place. This provides an important containment and frame for supervision. As before, this importantly parallels the early stages of the therapeutic process. There can be few therapists working who would not consider it important to fully explore with their new client the nature of the presenting issues, what they would want from counselling, and clearly define the nature of the relationship, including its limitations. If you are reading this and do not consider these 'starting points' to be important, perhaps a different career would be called for. The same is true for supervision.

Pause for reflection

1 What are the benefits of clear contracting at the beginning of counselling?
2 What are the dangers of contracting and how might these be managed?
3 In your own practice, what is the relationship between the nature of the containment in your supervision, and that of your work in therapy?

A place where work with clients can be explored and discussed

Within the relationship and process outlined above, and then supported by the clearly negotiated, agreed and reviewed boundaries of supervision, it then (and perhaps only then) becomes an appropriate space in which work with clients can be explored and discussed. This clearly includes all the types of risks that I have outlined in this book. So, it is important that we discuss with our supervisors the situational risks as they might arise (and be open to the possibility of them arising), but also keep in mind the other risks that might become apparent during the course of our work. As a therapist my anxiety might be particularly high if I am concerned about the potential suicide of one of my clients and supervision would be an important space for me to consider this fully and carefully, but the same is true for other risks that might be less obvious but that still present potential difficulty. Consider the following brief scenario.

Antony, Steve and Amanda

Steve has been seeing his client Antony for just over a year. They are of a similar age, get on very well and share a lot of perspectives about life. Steve has been very clear with Antony about the boundaries of their relationship (that it isn't a friendship), but they have also talked about how, in other situations, it might have been. Their work together has been very successful and both agree it is time for them to finish. A few months later Steve receives an email from Antony in which he acknowledges that ending counselling was more challenging than he anticipated given how well they got on. While he does not feel that he needs any further counselling at this stage, he would like to maintain contact with Steve on occasion, perhaps meeting up for coffee. Steve discusses this email with Amanda, his supervisor, and how he should respond.

In reading this scenario we might be very clear in our thinking about the issues of boundaries here and the importance of Steve not accepting Antony's suggestion. In that sense the risk of a boundary transgression is very clear. However, there are additional risks that Amanda was able to highlight and explore with Steve. To summarise, these were:

- The risk of saying yes and moving into a friendship with an ex-client
- The risk of saying no and of leaving Antony feeling rejected and hurt
- The risk of saying no and of leaving Steve feeling rejected and hurt
- The risk of the management of this process undermining the previous authenticity of their relationship and the work they did together
- The risk of Antony not feeling able to access counselling again in the future if it were needed, either with Steve or someone else
- The risk of Steve's unacknowledged feelings towards Amanda for holding the line over boundaries.

As we are often so aware, in many situations it is not necessarily *what* we do as therapists that may cause harm, but *how* we do it. While Steve needs to find a way of declining Antony's attempt at contact, it will be how he does that that will either have the potential to affirm all the work previously undertaken, or diminish it.

A relationship in which feedback can be given and received

It is clear through the issues we have already discussed how pivotal supervision is in helping us to reflect on the nature of risks as they present in therapy. Again, as in therapy itself, it is centrally important that the supervisory relationship is a sufficiently trustworthy one so that feedback can be given and received. Both supervisor and supervisee need to be able to consider their work together and discuss those aspects that positively contribute to the process, but that also have the potential to hinder it or become a risk. This is as true for the supervisory relationship itself as it is for those issues discussed during supervision, including direct client work and the wider functioning of the therapist as a professional. Sometimes the supervisor might become aware of concerns about the direct work of the therapist, or their wider professional actions, that need to be raised. These types of risks can be difficult to spot because they can emerge in the context of good practice, but point to the potential for harm, even though that is not intended. Consider the following scenario.

Jumana and Denise

Jumana is an experienced counsellor who has been working with children and young people for several years. She has seen her supervisor, Denise, for about four years and they have a good working alliance. Jumana's relationship with her partner abruptly and unexpectedly ended 14 months previously and it has been a difficult and challenging time for her. She has used supervision well and has also been for some individual therapy, which she found sometimes helpful. Jumana thoroughly enjoys her work and has agreed to begin counselling in two more schools. She mentioned this to Denise once the agreements were in place. She also has training commitments and sees a number of supervisees herself. Denise is concerned about Jumana's workload, that she might be 'throwing herself into her work' (as Jumana has talked about before) as a means of coping with her personal situation, and how that might impact on her work with the young people in school.

In a 'work hard' ethic that permeates the cultural level (both socially and professionally) it is not always easy to see working too hard as a risk. Jumana is evidently a responsible, caring and competent therapist who enjoys her work. However, if Denise is right, Jumana might be doing too much, with clear consequences for her but also her clients. The latter issue being that Jumana might not be as available to them emotionally or psychologically if she feels depleted herself. Denise might be in the best position to maintain a macro view of Jumana's work and commitments and, given the quality of their relationship and the clear boundaries that support it, could offer Jumana important feedback about her concerns and possibly bring into Jumana's awareness the potential risks of the situation.

A space for personal and professional development and the development of efficacy as a 'helper'

Risks that might be defined as personal are of enormous importance. It is for very good reasons that the ethical expectations of therapists from the majority of professional organisations associated with counselling and psychotherapy make specific reference to the need for practitioner self-care and self-regulation. It is not simply a case of 'How can we care for others if we cannot care for ourselves?', but 'What damage might I inadvertently cause to my clients or to myself if I fail to address my own needs appropriately?' These are challenging questions. It is my working assumption that the overwhelming majority of therapists are focused on the welfare of their clients and the appropriate meeting of their clients' needs and that they would not, under any circumstance, risk the value or efficacy of the therapeutic relationship through deliberate action. The danger of personal risks that remain unattended to in the context of therapy, however, is that the therapist, client, or both can experience harm as a consequence. Consider the following scenario.

Jack, Rebecca and Liam

Jack is 28 years old and has come to see Rebecca, his therapist, because of a relationship breakdown. This has been an acrimonious process for Jack with his ex-partner and he is left with feelings of anger, hurt and rejection. Two years before meeting Jack, Rebecca went through a similar experience with her partner at the time, a relationship that also ended acrimoniously – however the situations were reversed: Jack felt the 'wronged' party while Rebecca's ex-partner blamed her for the breakdown. Rebecca sought out counselling herself at the time and found this really useful. She talked with Liam, her supervisor, when she first began work with Jack about the similarities and the potential dangers of identification. In a supervision session Rebecca talked about Jack in quite an angry way, saying that he seemed unwilling to consider his part in the relationship difficulties and that it was unlikely a person could be entirely blame free.

On the face of it Rebecca has done everything right. She sought out support for herself at a time of difficulty, recognised the potential identification of problems between her and Jack's different situations, talked clearly and openly in supervision with Liam about the dangers, and progressed in working with Jack with thought and care. However, Liam has detected a dynamic in the way Rebecca is thinking about Jack's situation and how the issue of blame and responsibility has become an important focus for her. It might be that Jack is reluctant to explore difficult aspects of his own situation, but it is also possible that Rebecca is acting out her own hurt at having been blamed and needs Jack to accept responsibility to help her manage her own feelings. The dynamics are complex and potentially problematic, and supervision can provide the challenge to Rebecca to consider her own efficacy. The risk is that Jack leaves counselling with a construct and experience of his situation that is more reflective of Rebecca's perspective than his own.

A time during which professional standards, ethics and care can be scrutinised

Fundamentally it could be argued that working with risk in counselling and psychotherapy is about professional (and personal) standards, ethics and care. The biggest risk perhaps is that we pay no attention to risk at all and, by omission, cause or compound harm. Ethical frameworks and professional standards provide structures and mechanisms through which we can reflect on our own practice and the challenges that inevitably emerge from it. All of the scenarios outlined previously in this book centre around the management of our ethical responsibility to ourselves, our clients and the wider profession. At the time of writing the BACP are in the process of consulting on a revision to their Ethical Framework, to reflect the changing landscape of counselling and psychotherapy in the UK over the years since its first publication.

Professor Tim Bond, in leading the revision of the framework, has talked about the need for us to be ethically mindful; at its heart this is another way of describing ways of working with risk.

While we have a responsibility as practitioners to reflect on our own practice and behaviour – through the process of our 'internal supervisor' – there are also many other opportunities through which we can achieve the same outcome. Course attendance, reading books and journal articles, talking with peers, engagement with committees and working parties, etc., can all provide fruitful space to think about the ethical dimensions of our work. The role of supervision in the process, both in its own right but also in helping us to reflect on the other activities I outline here, cannot be overstated. The challenge is for us to strive to achieve an ethical engagement – or to be ethically mindful – in our responses to situations and dynamics in which risks are present.

Therapeutic transparency

The concept of therapeutic transparency relates to a number of risks outlined above that centre on ruptures both in the therapeutic relationship itself and in the actions surrounding and supporting the relationship, including communication. The level and nature of transparency will be informed by the model of practice, given that those working from a more psychodynamic or psychoanalytic frame will take a different position from those working humanistically, for example. The essence here, however, is practitioner congruence: that the way of being in therapy is led by the personal self (the qualities, characteristics and interpersonal style that shapes the way of being personally), but filtered through professional mechanisms and agreements. This is different from self-disclosure (where the therapist shares something of themselves or their lives with their clients), but is rather an integration of professional and personal ways of being.

Taking such a position can help to mitigate a range of risks that emerge in the personal and professional activities of therapy. From misunderstanding a client in a session through to a clumsy communication by email, the willingness to be transparent in that process, to accept responsibilities, to be humble and act with humility, to be corrected, to correct oneself, to accept moments of incompetence, to be open when we really don't know what to say next – to be fully present without a false veneer of being – can be profoundly important in acknowledging risks as they arise and working with them effectively to make them opportunities for change rather than hindrances to the process.

Professional action

The risk of complacency around our own competence can bring with it a potential to diminish our efficacy as a therapist. My own experience is that the moment I think I have it all sorted, that I know all that I need to know, something quickly comes along that makes me realise just how wrong I was and how little I do know. It can be a humbling experience but, as with many risks, it can also present an opportunity. The concept of 'professional action' is centred on the therapist's dynamic relationship with their own self and work, and how they can create sufficient professional movement so that competence becomes a dynamic and shifting entity. Continuing professional development teaches us new things, but it also reminds us that we need to keep learning; it irrigates an otherwise potentially barren landscape of ideas.

There are ranges of professional actions that contribute to our professional energy, which then translates into the lifeblood of therapy. Professional actions might include:

- Undertaking continuing professional development
- Helping develop policy and procedures, where needed (both in institutional settings and when working independently)
- Reading books and journal articles
- Reading or undertaking research
- Attending conferences
- Participating in webinars (online delivered consultations or seminars)
- Writing practitioner articles
- Watching relevant movies, training DVDs, etc.
- Undertaking online e-learning
- Participating in professional consultation groups
- Supervision
- Peer support and consultation
- Delivering training or teaching seminars
- Participating in local or national professional networks
- Writing practice guidance.

Each activity has the potential to contribute to your potency as a practitioner: it helps move you from the confines of the therapy room into a therapeutic community, with the opportunity to challenge and affirm practice and ensure you remain best placed to meet the needs of your clients.

Strategies for self-care

We talked previously about the impact of being a counsellor or psychotherapist on our personal self in the section on personal risks. While we might already engage in activities that positively contribute to our lives, the challenge here is also to do that in a way that is part of a strategy for self-care, so there is a balance between spontaneous acts, but also strategic ones too. There is a need to attend to:

- The therapeutic self: to avoid the dangers of vicarious trauma and self-care. Larcombe (2008: 287) writes of the need to: 'a) [establish] a method for gaining a sense of achievement; and b) [find] ways to disengage or create distance from clients between sessions'.
- The managerial self: we are all 'managers' of ourselves, regardless of working context. We need to pay attention to issues such as deadlines, workload, working environment, professional development and the management of change, for example. Larcombe (2008: 290–3) provides a helpful table outlining a range of issues with additional reflective questions.
- The career self: thinking about the longer-term process and how we envisage our careers developing and changing over time. This is important in ensuring our current practice does not become stagnant, but rather is part of a process of our own change and hope.

The list of self-care 'actions' could be almost limitless, depending on your own interests and things you enjoy. Each of us can usefully reflect on those things that positively contribute to our lives, and think about ways in which we can incorporate them more systematically in our daily routine. During a recent workshop looking at working with suicide risk, I asked the participants to list a number of things they enjoyed doing as part of their own self-care routines. I have incorporated a long, but edited list below, to help you think about things. The final aspect of such activities is that we do them mindful of the need to take care of ourselves. For example, we might enjoy going for a walk, but perhaps the next time you do a walk you tell yourself this is part of looking after your emotional and physical self and take each step being mindful of that intention.

- Music
- Sport
- Going for walks
- Taking breaks between clients
- Gardening
- Singing
- Reflexology
- Yoga
- Massage
- Personal or private journal
- Mindfulness/meditation

- Dance
- Alcohol (taken in moderation)
- Sailing
- A hug
- Time off
- Playing (being a child again)
- Holidays
- Reading
- Doing nothing
- Humour
- Theatre
- Chocolate
- Nature
- Cinema
- Cooking
- Seeing friends
- Surfing the net
- Surfing the sea
- Faith
- Pets
- Creative arts
- Personal therapy
- A partner
- Television
- Spending time with friends
- Sex
- Fresh air.

Pause for reflection

1 Make a list for yourself of things you enjoy doing.
2 Then note: (a) which things you are more likely to do spontane-ously; and (b) which things you might also be able to integrate into more conscious strategies for self-care.
3 Finally, make a note of those things that will prevent you from doing (2) above!

Chapter summary

In this chapter we have considered the different types of risk that may pre-sent during therapy, or around the wider process of therapy. Whereas previous chapters have discussed the implications of risks that might be

(Continued)

(Continued)

part of a client's presentation or response to distress, such as suicidal ideation or intent (situational risks), this chapter has highlighted other risks
associated with therapy. These are: those that might emerge as a consequence of, or during the therapeutic relationship (relational); those that
might become apparent as a consequence of organisational setting or following particular procedures (contextual); risks that relate specifically to
professional actions and behaviour of the therapist in the course of their
duties, which would include direct face-to-face work, online therapy and
the management of other ethical challenges (professional); and finally
those that relate to the wellbeing and functioning of the therapist themselves (personal).

The discussion has centred primarily around the use of supervision as an
integral part of the wider therapeutic process and how it can provide a safe
and appropriate place to explore good practice, ethical engagement and
help in providing a response to risk that leads to the best possible outcome.

10

POSITIVE RISK-TAKING

Chapter outline

This chapter will assert that all therapists engage in a collaborative positive risk-taking with clients. The term 'positive risk-taking' will be explored and defined, and scenarios will be outlined to demonstrate it 'in action'. The benefits of positive risk-taking for therapeutic change will be highlighted, with important factors for therapists to consider to ensure they and their clients remain safe, and that therapy itself remains ethical and respectful.

INTRODUCTION

Let me begin this chapter by presenting you with a scenario, the nature of which will be fairly familiar to many of you. The scenario relates to Darren.

> ### Darren
>
> Darren is 23 years old and has come to counselling on the advice of his GP. His relationship has broken down acrimoniously and he now has little contact with his ex-partner. He is socially isolated, with little family locally and very few friends. His GP has diagnosed Darren as having moderate to severe depression and has prescribed anti-depressants. In order to cope, Darren has been drinking heavily and, on occasions,
>
> *(Continued)*

(Continued)

taking illegal drugs. He is currently unemployed and has not been in work for several months. Darren struggles to talk about how he feels and his counsellor is aware that he seems to struggle to find an emotional language for expression. At points of frustration Darren will hit a wall and has, on occasions, seriously injured his knuckles and hand in doing so. Darren says that there are times when he just 'wants to go to sleep and not wake up', but he has not told his GP about this because his mother has mental health problems and was 'sectioned' on several occasions following her own suicide attempts. Darren will not give you permission to speak to his GP at this point but says that he really wants to make counselling work.

Quite simply, what will you do? You have possibly made a contract with Darren that limits confidentiality if you identify immediate concerns for your client's safety, such as around suicide risk, so you could legitimately break Darren's confidentiality, if necessary, to raise concerns with his GP. The risk of this is that any early therapeutic alliance is jeopardised and the potential is that Darren will not return to counselling and his social isolation will be further compounded. You could maintain Darren's confidentiality on the grounds that he is not expressing any clear suicidal intent, is expressing a desire for counselling to work and therefore has potential to make important changes in his life. As we discussed in Chapter 4, it is important that we are clear about our thinking for our clients, and ourselves, to help determine a collaborative outcome wherever possible. However, that does not detract from the ethical dilemma the counsellor has encountered. To summarise the specific risk factors – the factors that make suicide more likely – that Darren presents with:

- He is male
- He is young
- He has experienced a relationship breakdown
- He is socially isolated
- He is depressed
- He has started anti-depressants
- He has very few informal support options, such as family or friends
- He has been using alcohol and drugs
- He is unemployed
- He lacks a language for an easy expression of his emotions
- He sometimes self-harms by punching walls

- He has expressed some suicidal ideation
- He has a family history of suicide attempts
- He is refusing permission for you to help him access additional sources of support.

In terms of the protective factors, those factors that make suicide less likely would include:

- His GP is aware of most of Darren's problems (although not the suicidal ideation)
- He has come to a counselling session
- He has 'capacity' it seems, in that he can make informed decisions about his own life, even if they are unwise decisions
- He is optimistic about counselling
- He is willing to commit to counselling and will try to make the most of it
- He is sufficiently engaged with his counsellor at this stage, suggesting the development of an early therapeutic alliance
- He has the potential for change
- His suicidal ideation is not yet specific intent, as far as we know
- He is not suicidal all of the time
- He has not already killed himself, suggesting some desire to live.

Pause for reflection

1 Having looked at the risk and protective factors, which ones do you think are key in making a decision about Darren?
2 Would you break his confidentiality, or maintain his confidentiality, at least at this stage?

I have been training counsellors, psychotherapists, nurses, psychologists and psychiatrists, etc. for many years in relation to working with suicide risk and often present this sort of dilemma for discussion. While I don't claim this to be a rigorous evidence base, of the thousands of therapists I have worked with in the training environment the majority would not break Darren's confidentiality. We discussed in Chapter 4 how we can reach such decisions ethically, but what is key here is that all those who would choose not to break Darren's confidentiality are working proactively with a presenting risk. By this I mean they are aware of the risks, have made a collaborative judgement with Darren (hopefully) that they will maintain confidentiality at this stage at least, and will not disclose the risk factors to the GP as this would go against Darren's known wishes. They have judged, on balance, that the protective factors are sufficient to mitigate the risk factors. Inevitably therefore, they are engaging in positive risk-taking.

I would assert here that this sort of decision-making process takes place many times a day, every day, every week, every month in every therapy environment. Counsellors and psychotherapists work confidentially with clients who present as at risk, such as risk of suicide, all the time, otherwise the confidentiality of a large number of people who attended for therapy would be broken and they would be referred on, and this is not the case. I use the term 'positive' in this context because the rationale for such a decision is typically based on the potential for positive client change. In this scenario, it will be hoped that as Darren has engaged in counselling, his suicidal thoughts will reduce over time and, with support, he will begin to make important changes in his life to promote his wellbeing.

The outcome of this situation is difficult to predict and, at best, we can only use the information we have to make informed best judgements of potential outcome. If the belief was that Darren would almost certainly kill himself then it is likely the counsellor would inform the GP of the risk, partly because they have contracted to and partly because they have an ethical duty to work to safeguard the client's wellbeing. We can take Darren's scenario and translate it into a range of settings, such as schools, other youth services, third sector services, education and health; the dilemmas are the same. Working with school counsellors for example, I am very aware of the tension between maintaining counselling confidentiality and safeguarding procedures (we explored this in more detail in Chapter 7). Sometimes schools will require their counsellors to raise *any* safeguarding concerns with the relevant person in school, even if the young person would prefer the counsellor not to. This might include even when a young person indicates low-level suicidal thoughts, but no intent – sometimes just talking about suicide is sufficient to invoke safeguarding procedures in some settings. Counsellors and psychotherapists find themselves in these situations making very difficult decisions about respecting the client's autonomy (if the young person is competent to understand therapy) and working within procedural expectations. Situations might include:

- Working with suicidal ideation where the intent is uncertain and the client is committed to therapy
- Working when a client is self-injuring or self-harming in a chaotic and unmanaged way
- Where there are safeguarding concerns but it is not clear whether it is necessary to take action

- Where child protection concerns are suspected, but not clear, and the client says they will do something about it themselves
- Where there are concerns about a client's deteriorating health or general wellbeing, perhaps through lack of self-care or an eating disorder, for example
- Where there is concern about emerging mental health distress, such as psychosis
- Where a client talks of angry outbursts and rage against another, and makes threats of harm, but says they are not likely to act on these thoughts.

These situations give some indication as to how risk factors might present in such a way that therapists might consider not acting immediately but perhaps see how the situation develops or resolves. An interesting common factor in most of them is where the situation is not clear-cut: a lack of clarity over possible outcome and the potential for positive change.

If we go back to Darren, the wisdom of his counsellor's decision to respect his confidentiality and not inform the GP will only become apparent in hindsight. If Darren engages in counselling, his suicidal thoughts reduce and things begin to improve it would seem to be a very sensible and facilitative decision. If Darren ends his life soon after the session it would seem to be a misguided and poor decision: the decision is the same but its efficacy is defined by subsequent events. The answer here, of course, is for counsellors and psychotherapists to be trained to predict the future so as to mitigate all such uncertainty. Until a 'Predicting the Future' module is launched on a training programme and proven to be successful, we must assume that we cannot predict the future and can only act on the information we have available to us at that point. We might say that there is risk in taking the risk. It would be professionally much safer if we decided not to positively risk-take collaboratively with our clients and, if in doubt, pass on our concerns regardless of our client's wishes. We might argue, however, that such a stance would undermine important ethical principles that fuel the very heart and soul of our work; as therapists we inevitably and always work with uncertainty.

POSITIVE RISK-TAKING IN PRACTICE: OKAY OR A TABOO?

We have used the scenario of a client with suicidal thoughts to illustrate the process of how we reach a situation where we might positively take risks. However, the concept of positive risk-taking can be realised in a number of ways in therapy. If we begin by thinking more generally and away from therapy for a moment, it is useful to reflect on the debates that take place in society about risk. For example, should children be allowed to go out to play in the local woods on their own and run the risk of assault? Should they be allowed to climb trees, crawl through pipes, play near building sites, climb on high walls? Should adults be allowed to smoke in their own home, their car, in a restaurant? Should we be allowed to take risks with our health through poor diets, lack of exercise, taking supplements and so on? The list of risks we negotiate as a society is almost endless, with high passion at each polarity of the discussion. Another example, but also a good metaphor for this dilemma, comes in the increase in sales of anti-bacterial sprays, wipes, gloves, clothes, etc. and prescriptions for antibiotics. Some would argue that this is progress and the use of such things helps in the prevention of disease and contributes to good health. Others, however, argue that by sanitising the world around us and not allowing ourselves to be exposed to the risk of germs and lack of cleanliness we ultimately undermine our resilience to cope with the world and, paradoxically, increase the risk of disease because we no longer possess the physical wherewithal to fight it ourselves. Should we clean away the dirt, or build resilience to it? It is a metaphor that threads throughout the whole debate around positive risk-taking, including in the counselling and psychotherapy context. There are a number of potential advantages to be experienced if a client is helped to negotiate their way through a difficult and risky experience. These can include the following aspects:

- Collaboratively working with another around risk can bring about a sense of connection and further enhance the therapeutic alliance
- It can provide the client with an opportunity for insight or self-understanding, as the nature of the presenting difficulties is often more immediate or accessible
- Negotiating a path through risk can help build confidence in coping strategies and contribute to a developing emotional resilience
- Therapists can help clients reflect on the nature of their change process and bridge that insight into other situations, including those that might contain other risks, and those that don't
- Can contribute to relational depth
- Can affirm practitioner competence and develop confidence.

In some ways it is difficult to envisage not positively taking risks in the context of counselling and psychotherapy, given the uncertainties and unknowns with which we work all the time. With every client, and in many situations, we are both working with not knowing how future plans and hopes will develop, or what new crises might arise. This is the nature and flow of the therapeutic process. The context of risk as we are exploring it here is more related to the possibility of specific events or the emergence of potential negative outcomes and how we might work within that context. While talking about our attitudes to cleanliness might seem unrelated, it sits on the same continuum of how we approach risk more generally. In this respect, how we work with risk in counselling and psychotherapy is going to be strongly influenced by our own attitude to risk. Even where working policy is more at the prescriptive rather than general end of the spectrum, it is often our interpretation of the situation and how the policy applies to it that matters. As we have outlined with Darren, our attitude to risk will profoundly shape and influence our relationship to risk, which will be present in our direct work with clients.

THERAPEUTIC STEPS IN POSITIVE RISK-TAKING

Essentially it is my assertion here that while positive risk-taking is per-haps embedded in the very nature of the therapeutic process at a general level, there are more discrete situations and dynamics that might afford an appropriate and ethical opportunity to work specifi-cally with risk rather than to simply close those situations down. However, the client's wellbeing sits at the heart of this process and I am not advocating a situation where counsellors and psychotherapists make unilateral decisions about how best to proceed. There are several therapeutic steps I would suggest are helpful in determining responses to situations involving risk. These are:

- The client has the capacity to understand the nature and extent of the risk as it presents
- The client is willing and able to work collaboratively with the therapist around risk
- The therapist understands the nature and extent of the risk as it presents
- The therapist is willing and able to work collaboratively with the client around risk
- Any actions and agreements are made within the context of any con-tract in place for therapy, or variations are clearly negotiated and agreed to beforehand and remain ethically informed
- No actions or agreements should disregard any existing policy or prac-tice expectation around how to respond to risk situations

- Any actions are regularly reviewed and fully explored in supervision and line management, if appropriate
- All actions and agreements are recorded, in writing, or in a format accessible to the client while respecting their confidentiality.

In looking at each of these steps in a little more detail, I will make reference to Alistair to help illustrate these practice steps 'in action'.

Alistair

Alistair is 18 years old and has been attending counselling because of panic attacks. He has been more agitated over recent sessions and brings along a diary he has been keeping. It is a book full of scribbles and ripped paper, with some pen drawings of monsters. Alistair tells his counsellor that the voices in his head tell him to draw these things and the only way he can shut the voices up is to cut himself. Jenni, Alistair's counsellor has agreed a contract of confidentiality limited by concerns of risk to self and others. The agency policy (a third sector agency) recognises that risk will be present in sessions and facilitates therapists to make informed decisions, with their supervisors, about ways of working. However, the policy does expect therapists to work within the context of the contracts made.

The client has the capacity to understand the nature and extent of the risk as it presents

We discussed the concept of mental capacity in earlier chapters and explored the importance of the therapist determining the client's capacity, or lack of capacity, in making decisions for themselves, in the context of the therapist's competence to do so. This is important in working proactively with risk, in that the client must be able to understand the nature of the risk (what it is about the particular situation or dynamic that presents risk), as well as its extent (what the consequences of the risk situation occurring might be). As in any situation, it is essential that the client is able to fully appreciate the situation or dynamic as it presents so that they can decide the best way to proceed. The therapist not taking this consideration into account leads to the potential for harm and unethical practice.

If we consider Alistair (above), in many situations self-injury would be part of a client's presentation that might not typically lead to breaking the client's confidentiality. Jenni might understand the client's actions as ways of self-support, albeit self-destructive, that could improve as the client finds alternative ways of helping and expressing themselves. However, there is a strong suggestion that Alistair is experiencing acute mental health crisis, and possibly early onset psychosis. While Jenni would not diagnose Alistair's mental health state, she would be expected to recognise Alistair's severe vulnerability. What is uncertain in this situation is Alistair's level of mental capacity because of his distress. In this context Jenni would need to decide whether Alistair was able to work with the risk to himself of the self-injury – understanding its nature and extent – or whether Alistair was temporarily unable to do so, which would make working with the risk without recourse to further specialist support questionable. The client's mental capacity is crucial here – as is determining it if Jenni is unsure.

The client is willing and able to work collaboratively with the therapist around risk

Whether the client will work collaboratively with the therapist around risk is partly dependent on their capacity to do so, but not entirely. It is essential that positive risk-taking is not 'done to' the client, but is instead a collaborative process that both are willing and able to engage in. While therapy is often crucial in supporting a client's move from a place of difficulty to one that is stronger and more resilient, therapy typically is only 50 or 60 minutes per week in a client's life. Essentially, positive risk-taking will be a process that falls more on the client than the therapist in terms of action and responsibility. As such, the client must be willing and able to work within these parameters. Other factors might include: the quality of the therapeutic alliance; the client's available support systems and their willingness to access them; the client's psychological mindedness; their willingness to take active steps to support themselves; and the level of trust between client and therapist.

If Alistair is deemed by Jenni to potentially be temporarily lacking in capacity to make informed decisions for himself (and to understand the nature and extent of the risk he faces), then it would be unethical to proceed as if he did have capacity. Instead, Jenni should take the necessary steps to activate additional assessment and intervention. If Jenni believes Alistair does have capacity to make informed decisions for himself, she then needs to explore with Alistair how he wishes to proceed and whether he feels able to work proactively in counselling while the risk is still evident, which will necessitate an exploration that covers the types of factors outlined in the previous paragraph.

The therapist understands the nature and extent of the risk as it presents

The two areas above as discussed in relation to clients are equally applicable to therapists. We might assume here that in virtue of being in practice therapists have mental capacity. While it might be an obvious statement it is perhaps worth stating that without mental capacity, therapists should not be in practice. However, having mental capacity does not necessarily mean that the therapist inevitably understands the nature and extent of risks when they present. As we have discussed previously, the nature of risk often changes in the process of individual interpretation that, in turn, is informed by a number of factors, including: the therapist's relationship to risk; their own experience of managing risk in their own lives; family patterns around risk (such as risk avoidant or risk-taking); their emotional resilience; experience as a therapist; model of therapy; and other personal beliefs.

Jenni might understand that Alistair's mental health state is vulnerable and, as such, he might have less ability to manage his own self-injuring and thus be at greater risk of serious harm, or instead she might have little experience in working with such issues and not appreciate the potential for greater risk. In this latter context Jenni might therefore assume that Alistair's self-injury is part of an understandable coping strategy that does not require particular additional attention. In working proactively with risk it is therefore essential that we reflect carefully on our own capacity to work with certain types of presentations and use supervision to fully explore the limits of our own understanding.

The therapist is willing and able to work collaboratively with the client around risk

Linked with the points made above about understanding are those considerations that relate more to our own personal capacity to hear and respond effectively to certain situations. Following the death of one of my own clients through suicide, which I have described in more detail elsewhere (Reeves, 2010), I struggled for a while to contain my anxiety in response to any expression of suicide by other clients, regardless of how low the level of risk might have been. My emotional resilience had been undermined and, as such, my ability to work collaboratively with clients around risk was depleted. We must again use supervision, as well as other reflective opportunities, to consider how well we are able to respond to issues that might be personally very difficult for us to hear.

In the case scenario above, Jenni might feel confident in working with the types of issues Alistair is struggling with, including his self-injury, or might have little experience or training in working with mental health issues. As such, she might be confident, assured, containing and affirming in her relationship with Alistair, or might instead be tentative, anxious, reactive and overwhelmed. I have also written elsewhere (Reeves, 2013a) about how our attitude to self-injury can shape our capacity to hear it. For example, it might be that Jenni simply doesn't understand why someone might cut themselves, or perhaps might not approve of it. All of these factors will inform how well Jenni is able to enter into a collaborative process around Alistair's risk that will, in turn, inform Alistair's willingness to work in a collaborative process too: the dynamic is often a cyclical one.

Any actions and agreements are made within the context of any contract in place for therapy, or variations are clearly negotiated and agreed to beforehand and remain ethically informed

Beyond the immediacy of the therapeutic dynamic is the context in which the relationship takes place. All counselling and psychotherapy takes place in a context: it never happens in a vacuum. The context will vary but will always shape and inform the nature of therapy. This is an important consideration in this therapeutic step, and also the next one we will discuss, because context will be important in defining the nature of the contract agreed for therapy, including independent practice. When therapy begins we take time and consideration to outline the parameters of the therapeutic work (time, length of session, frequency, cost, nature of the confidentiality offered, including limitations, and so on). This is the basis on which therapy begins and is sustained and provides a fundamental bedrock for the development of the therapeutic alliance and the level of trust. Decisions about how best to respond to risk situations or dynamics as they emerge during therapy need to be informed by the original contract. It is questionable practice ethically for contracts simply to be forgotten or overridden for the sake of a particular type of intervention. That is not to say that contracts might not need to be re-negotiated during the course of therapy, as good contracts are reviewed regularly, but this should be done carefully, clearly and collaboratively and preferably not in response to a particular situation or dynamic but rather as a consequence of an experience of the process of therapy.

Jenni's contract with Alistair is boundaried by risk of harm to self or others. We have discussed in various chapters previously that meeting this limitation might be problematic as it could involve us breaking confidentiality in response to any potential for harm, no matter how minimal or transient. Jenni would have talked through what this particular limitation might mean in her setting for Alistair's confidentiality and would need to act accordingly. It would not be appropriate for Jenni to state to Alistair that while they had agreed this limitation at the beginning, she had now changed her mind and all would remain confidential. Whether or not to share her concerns about Alistair's mental health and his potential for serious harm must be informed by these agreed boundaries.

No actions or agreements should disregard any existing policy or practice expectation around how to respond to risk situations

In the same vein as the points made above about contracts, actions around working with risk need to be informed by any policies or procedural guidelines in place. This is an important consideration, given that my own research has suggested that where counsellors do not agree with an organisational policy around suicide, they are more likely to ignore it rather than challenge it (Reeves and Mintz, 2001). It is essential that we work within the parameters of any policies that inform our work as it leaves the work, and us, very vulnerable if things do not work out as planned. This can be challenging if we do not agree with the philosophy that underpins the policy or it directs us to work in a way that is inconsistent with how we would prefer to work. Of course, any policy that directs us to work in a way that is contrary to any ethical directions we have signed up to needs to be challenged openly. Short of that, however, the organisation is very influential in how decisions are made in the counselling process.

Jenni's employing organisation is not untypical of many outside statutory services. That is, therapists are encouraged to make their own informed decisions with clients about how to respond to risk situations, in consultation with supervisors, but ultimately must place the wellbeing of the client and compliance with the agreed contract at the forefront of the decision-making process. How Jenni and Alistair decide to proceed must therefore be based on a sound rationale for practice that is informed by all key factors present in the situation. This is discussed more fully in those chapters that discuss situational risks in more detail.

Any actions are regularly reviewed and fully explored in supervision and line management, if appropriate

There are two key components of this therapeutic step: the importance of reviewing; and the centrality of the importance of supervision and line management consultation. With respect to the latter, supervision has to sit right at the heart of any considerations around working with risk. This provides the practitioner with the best possible opportunity to stand back from their own perspective and consider all key aspects, including the practitioner's own views and personal responses to the risk. Likewise, in addition to supervision there may be an opportunity to discuss the implications of potential decisions with a line manager, or with colleagues and peers (bearing in mind the client's confidentiality). This is more likely to happen when therapy takes place in an organisational context, but it is not uncommon for independent practitioners to establish appropriate peer supervision networks in addition to their own formal supervision arrangements. A point of good practice here is that all decisions that pertain to a best response to risk should, wherever possible and feasible, be taken in consultation with another to help mitigate personal responses or professional pressures that might influence the decision in an unhelpful way.

The former point above is concerned with the importance of reviewing. Decisions are best if they can adapt and respond to the changing circumstances of practice. This is particularly true when proactively working with risk situations, given that the situation may well change from week to week. As part of the process it is important for therapists to put time aside with their clients, supported through supervisory consultation, to review the outcomes of previous decisions made and how best things can move forward from that point.

Jenni needs to consider all of these factors in her work with Alistair. Supervision will help her consider her thoughts about the possibility of Alistair's early onset psychosis, or indeed consider other potential explanations for his behaviour (perhaps drug or alcohol use, for example). If she and Alistair decide (because she considers he has the mental capacity to do so) to continue with their work for the time being in the hope that things might improve, it will be important that this decision is carefully reviewed on a week-by-week basis to ensure it still continues to meet Alistair's needs.

All actions and agreements are recorded, in writing, or in a format accessible to the client while respecting their confidentiality

Finally, we turn to the importance of recording any actions taken and the processes of decision making that informed those actions. There are several reasons for this:

- Careful records of decisions help provide a clear audit trail of what was decided, by whom, and when
- Records should ensure that all factors that were taken into account in making the decision are detailed, such as the risk factors, the protective

factors, the client's mental capacity and the rationale for the outcome

- Such details provide a time-line of action so that interventions are transparent and appropriate
- Therapists can use such records to help inform supervisory discussions, or consultation with a line manager, for example
- Records of previous sessions can help inform the review process
- Records help indicate how policies or practice guidance have been taken into account and followed
- Records help bridge decisions made in practice to the contracted parameters for therapy
- Records help provide an opportunity for a practitioner to articulate practice in the event of client complaint
- Records can help the client, once they have accessed them, in the event of needing to make a complaint
- Appropriate records essentially provide a justification for practice decisions.

All of those points would help Jenni in her work with Alistair and contribute to an appropriate, trusting and well sustained therapeutic alliance.

Chapter summary

In this chapter we have considered the concept of positive risk-taking, in the context of risk often being defined only in the light of possible negative outcome. While risk is often associated with negative outcome, such as harm to the client or another person, there are potential therapeutic advantages of working proactively and positively with risk situations as this can lead to growth, insight and change. However, there are important caveats in positive risk-taking, including the importance of the client's and therapist's understanding of the nature and extent of risk, the client's mental capacity to make informed decisions about their therapy, and other influences that might shape and inform practice. A number of therapeutic steps are outlined to help practitioners work ethically in the light of risk, move away from the idea of defensive practice (where practice decisions are made primarily for the value of self-protection), and embrace the possibilities that working proactively with risk can bring about.

11

CONCLUSION: BRINGING IT TOGETHER

Chapter outline

The purpose of this chapter is to bring together the key messages from the book, summarising the areas of risk that might present in counselling and psychotherapy and offering some good practice indicators. The chapter will additionally contain some useful reflective questions to help you to consider your own practice and how you work with risk, as well as potential areas for development.

INTRODUCTION

In approaching writing this text I wondered what was to be gained in producing a book that looked at risk more generally and how might that contribute to professional practice. I deliver lots of training around working with specific areas of risk and am very aware of how risk is often responded to with a sense of dread and foreboding by many practitioners. The research evidence seems to support this too, with findings talking of practitioner anxiety, fear, anger, sense of impotence and distress, all in response to facing risk in client work.

It is certainly true, and something I know from my own practice, that working with risk can be daunting and frightening at times, but it seemed to me that there was also an opportunity potentially being lost here. I worked for many years in a mental health crisis service and, as a consequence, learnt over time and from many people that risk and a point of crisis can also bring with it real opportunities for insights, development, understanding and change. Indeed, for some, it can be the only time when such a depth of insight might be possible, before the defences and barriers are put in place again. Our task as therapists, regardless of theoretical orientation and practice setting, is ultimately about supporting and facilitating our clients through greater understanding and, if that turns out to be the right thing for them, change. I add this caveat on at the end because a good therapeutic outcome does not always equate to change, but rather a different and more informed way of continuing with the status quo.

To work with risk as an opportunity however, we need to understand its essence and process so that it becomes part of therapy rather than a hindrance to therapy. To achieve this takes time, reflection, skill, collaboration, determination, a little bit of luck and a bit more bravery. Someone once spoke of working with risk as 'flying by the seat of your pants'. While it can feel that way, I would beg to differ over whether risk needs to be such a daunting, disorientating and 'out of control' sort of process. It certainly can be, but the task here is to face risk squarely, alongside our clients, so that we can work collaboratively to mitigate its worst potential and harness its opportunities.

RISK: A PHILOSOPHICAL POSITION

We defined risk as:

> (Exposure to) the possibility of loss, injury, or other adverse or unwelcome circumstance; a chance or situation involving such a possibility [or]
>
> To act in such a way as to bring about the possibility of (an unpleasant or unwelcome event) [or]
>
> to take a risk, be bold or daring.

While two of these statements focus on the detrimental aspects of risk, the third talks of being bold and daring. The position in this last statement is about 'taking' a risk, which implies an active taking control of a situation, rather than a passive recipient of whatever might happen. It is that resourceful positioning I have advocated throughout this book. I do not encourage unilateral risk-taking, where the therapist on a flight of fancy heads off down a road that is indeed bold and daring, but does so without the client's understanding and consent. That would, at best, be *doing to* a client rather than *doing with* and, at worst, be potentially unethical, placing the client in a position of potential harm. Rather, I advocate that we use risk as a discursive opportunity to deepen the therapeutic alliance – the relational depth – so that we can truly experience each other's existence and together agree a way of negotiating the challenges that have arisen. We can only do this if we are willing to sit side by side and talk about the really difficult things.

The challenge therefore, of the points made throughout this book, is that we should be willing to be brave and to name the things that might frighten us most, whether that be the potential for our client's suicide; a life-threatening chaos around a deteriorating pattern of self-injury; the protection of children and young people; safeguarding the wellbeing of children, young people and vulnerable adults; the potential for violence and so on. Being willing and able to name the otherwise unsayable, and doing so, opens new narrative opportunities. In this light I suggest an active participation in the process of risk and suggest it as a three-dimensional engagement rather than a two-dimensional aspect of a client's presentation that we must simply assess and respond to. As with our clients, risk can be something we *do with*, rather than being *done to*.

Pause for reflection

1 Think of times in your personal life when you have had to face a risk.
2 What were the dangers of this risk, and what were the opportunities?
3 In negotiating this risk did you feel that you were depleted by it, or were able to grow because of it? What made the biggest difference to you?

THE MANY FACES OF RISK

The structure of this book has addressed key areas of risk as we have progressed. I have talked about risks across five primary domains:

- Situational: risks that relate to specific potential events or situations
- Relational: risks that emerge in the therapeutic relationship
- Contextual: risks that relate to the context in which therapy takes place
- Professional: risks that relate to professional behaviour or action
- Personal: risks to the wellbeing of the practitioner.

We can all too often only focus on the situational risks – suicide, self-harm, violence to others – and miss other risks as they present and then pass us by. These particularly include risks that might emerge from the therapeutic process itself; those relational risks that speak of the dynamic between our clients and us and that can, when fully engaged with and explored, potentially open real opportunities for a different way of seeing things. Then there are the risks that pertain to our own wellbeing – vicarious trauma and burnout. As I have said earlier in the text, it is those of us who imagine that such an outcome is highly unlikely to happen who are at most risk. Then, of course, there are the contextual risks, those that relate to the settings in which we work and the unique and shared aspects of the professional structures of practice that can both help and hinder therapy, such as policies, procedures and ill-thought-out practices.

I have therefore tried to be as inclusive as possible in detailing the sorts of risks that relate to the practice of counselling and psychotherapy and to show how different risks can be present at different times. In doing so I hope I have been able to illustrate how, in engaging in risk in different ways, we already have competence in negotiating difficulties and turning potentially bad situations into better ones.

Pause for reflection

1 Think of the five domains of risk we have discussed: situational; relational; contextual; professional; and personal – identify one risk in each domain that relates to your: (a) personal world; and (b) professional world.
2 Of the five areas, which ones are easier for you to negotiate, and which ones the more challenging? Why?
3 Can you think of any additional domains not included here that would relate to risk?

BREATH, GROUNDING AND COLLABORATION

I have called this last section 'Breath, grounding and collaboration' because, for me, these typify key characteristics that can help us work effectively with risk while safeguarding our clients and ourselves; they apply to our clients and ourselves equally. By breath I refer to the capacity to support ourselves with our own anxieties: being able to breathe into our anxieties so that we don't become overwhelmed by them. By grounding I refer to a point of anchorage and safety, and being able to engage with a sense of stability and trust. By collaboration I mean: working effectively with risk should always equate to working effectively with our clients so that we are truly alongside. With these three things in place we give ourselves the best opportunity to make sense of the difficulties inherent in a situation and find a way through them.

There are some useful points to remember as we work with risk that can further help promote our client's and our own wellbeing. I will explore them across the five domains I previously outlined for risk itself.

Situational

- Being open to the possibility of risk in our clients, even when such risk might not always be apparent
- Knowing that risk is not always spoken but may still be present in the room
- Understanding that risk can be because of potential action, but also thought, feeling and the client's physical self
- Being prepared to ask direct, straightforward, open but empathic questions
- Being willing, once the questions have been asked, to continue to explore issues rather than turn away from them
- Remembering that therapy represents only a short time in a client's week and that working with risk is always about identifying and engaging with the client's resources for self-support
- Knowing that because of distress clients may not always have capacity to engage with managing the risk on their own
- Knowing that responding to the risk, even if it is without the client's consent, can be the most respectful thing to do
- Remembering that, if in doubt, act.

Relational

- Understanding that even if the risk relates to something outside of the therapy, the mechanism for exploration is a relational one
- One of the key factors in responding effectively to risk is the robustness of the therapeutic alliance
- Some risks may be hard for the client to engage with because of the shame associated with them, which may be experienced because of the relational dynamic
- Some risks might sit in the transferential or countertransferential dynamic
- Relationships that take place within clearly articulated and negotiated boundaries provide the best opportunity to work with challenges when they arise

- Holding the boundaries also requires commensurate skill and attention so that clients are not left damaged or rejected
- Risks that emerge relationally can also be responded to relationally, where possible and appropriate.

Contextual

- Having a clear understanding of the ethical principles that inform your practice provides for the best risk management environment
- Ensuring that service provision is fair and equitable and embedded within the client need
- Independent practice requires considerable care and attention in ensuring it is sufficiently robust to withstand the risks that might emerge in the therapeutic process
- Policies and procedures must be comprehensive yet accessible, directive yet open for interpretation, robust but flexible
- The setting must be suited to the delivery of therapy, and the wellbeing of both the client and the therapist must be at the forefront of the structure of the service
- Like therapy, services must be open to the process of reviewing, particularly in the light of risks as they present and how they are responded to.

Professional

- Continuing professional development provides not only an opportunity for skills development, but also to learn from the experience of others as they have faced and managed risks
- Membership of a professional body provides an external ethical and accountable structure within which practice can be located
- An external ethical and accountable structure provides for some containment at points of anxiety and concern, and gives an opportunity to consult and reflect
- Supervision provides an appropriate and confidential space for the therapist to explore dilemmas, identify risks and consider collaboratively (thus paralleling the therapeutic process) different ways forward
- Supervision can additionally provide an opportunity for challenge to the therapist and so help them either work proactively with the risk, or to know when a limit has been reached.

Personal

- We are not immune from our own trauma and burnout – thinking we are immune makes it more likely
- We will take into our client sessions every aspect of us – our tensions, worries, challenges and problems as well as our own risks

- We need to ensure there is reflective space to be aware of our own aspects so that they are not acted out in a session
- We need to reflect on our capacity to work with risk: whether we are risk averse or risk tolerant, and how that might change over time and in response to different circumstances
- Self-care does not just happen – we have to work at it and establish a mechanism for it, and review it regularly.

FINAL THOUGHTS

I hope in reading this book you have been prompted to reflect on your attitude to risk and how you identify and respond to it in practice. I hope it has affirmed what you already know about yourself as a practitioner, and opened new doors for further consideration and exploration. We cannot eradicate risk from therapeutic practice and, arguably, if we achieved that goal we would also eradicate the heart and soul of what we do. The joy, and challenge, of counselling and psychotherapy is that it takes us into the unknown, the unfamiliar, the uncertain, the occasionally worrying and the often rewarding. Risk is a component that facilitates that process and we might reflect on how we can embrace it, and engage with it, with enthusiasm and energy.

REFERENCES

Adams, M. (2013) *The Myth of the Untroubled Therapist: Private Life, Professional Practice*. London: Routledge.

American Psychiatric Association (2013) *Diagnostic and Statistical Manual of Mental Disorders* (5th edn). Arlington, VA: American Psychiatric Publishing.

Appleby, L., Shaw, J., Sherratt, J., Amos, T., Robinson, J. and McDonnell, R. (2001) *Safety First: Five Year Report of the National Confidential Inquiry into Suicide and Homicide by People with a Mental Illness*. London: HMSO.

Aoun, S. (1999) 'Deliberate self-harm in rural Western Australia: Results of an intervention study', *Australian and New Zealand Journal of Mental Health Nursing*, 8(2): 65–73.

Araminta, T. (2000) 'Dialectical behavior therapy: A qualitative study of therapist and client experience', *Dissertation Abstracts International: Section B: The Sciences and Engineering*, 61(1-B): 520.

Babiker, G. and Arnold, L. (1997) *The Language of Injury: Comprehending Self-Mutilation*. Oxford: Wiley-Blackwell.

BACP (2010) 'Updates: BACP policy and position statement: December 2009', *Children and Young People*, March: 46.

BACP (2013) *Ethical Framework for Good Practice in Counselling and Psychotherapy*. Lutterworth: British Association for Counselling and Psychotherapy.

Barker, M. (2013) 'A phenomenological exploration of counsellor's use of social networks: the implications for the boundaries and self-disclosure'. Unpublished dissertation, University of Chester.

Battle, A.O., Battle, M.V. and Tolley, E.A. (1993) 'Potential for suicide and aggression in delinquents at juvenile court in a southern city', *Suicide and Life Threatening Behavior*, 23(3): 230–43.

Beulow, G. and Range, L.M. (2001) 'No-suicide contracts among college students', *Death Studies*, 25: 583–92.

Bond, T. and Mitchels, B. (2014) *Confidentiality and Record Keeping in Counselling and Psychotherapy* (2nd edn). London: Sage

Carroll, M. (1996) *Counselling Supervision: Theory, Skills and Practice*. London: Sage.

Comtois, K.A. and Linehan, M.M. (2006) 'Psychosocial treatments of suicidal behaviors: A practice-friendly review', *Journal of Clinical Psychology: In Session*, 62(2): 161–70.

Cooper, M. (2008) *Essential Research Findings in Counselling and Psychotherapy: The Facts are Friendly*. London: Sage.

Cooper, M. and Reeves, A. (2012) 'The role of randomised-controlled trials in developing an evidence-base for counselling and psychotherapy', *Counselling and Psychotherapy Research*, 12(4): 303–7.

Craig, C.D. and Sprang, G. (2010) 'Compassion satisfaction, compassion fatigue, and burnout in a national sample of trauma treatment therapists', *Anxiety, Stress and Coping: An International Journal*, 23(3): 319–39.

Craigen, L.M. (2006) 'A qualitative investigation of the counselling experiences of college-aged women with a history of self-injury', *Dissertation Abstracts International Section A: Humanities and Social Sciences*, 67(3-A): 845.

Cunningham, K., Wolbert, R. and Lillie, B. (2004) 'It's about me solving my problems: Clients' assessments of dialectical behavior therapy', *Cognitive and Behavioral Practice*, 11(2): 248–56.

Daniels, D. and Jenkins, P. (2010) *Therapy with Children: Children's Rights, Confidentiality and the Law* (2nd edn). London: Sage.

De Leo, D., Burgis, S., Bertolote, J.M., Kerkof, A.J. and Bille-Brahe, U. (2006) 'Definitions of suicidal behaviour: Lessons learnt from the WHO/EURO multicentre study', *Crisis*, 27: 4–15.

Department of Health (2014) *Statistical Update on Suicide*. London: Crown Copyright. Available at: www.gov.uk/government/uploads/system/uploads/attachment_data/file/278120/Suicide_update_Jan_2014_FINAL_revised.pdf (accessed 7 August 2014).

Department of Health and Home Office (2000) *No Secrets: Guidance on Developing and Implementing Multi-agency Policies and Procedures to Protect Vulnerable Adults from Abuse*. London: Department of Health.

Despenser, S. (2005) 'The personal safety of the therapist', *Psychodynamic Practice*, 11(4): 429–46.

Douglas, K.S., Ogloff, J.R.P., Nicholls, T.L. and Grant, I. (1999) 'Assessing risk for violence among psychiatric patients: The HCR-20 violence risk assessment scheme and the Psychopathy Checklist: Screening Version', *Journal of Consulting and Clinical Psychology*, 67(6): 917–30.

Ellerby, M. (2007) *On Anti-psychiatry*. Brentwood: Chipmunka publishing.

Evans, C., Connell, J., Barkham, M., Margison, F., McGrath, G., Mellor-Clark, J. and Audin, K. (2002) 'Towards a standardised brief outcome measure: Psychometric properties and utility of the CORE-OM', *British Journal of Psychiatry*, 180: 51–60.

Evans, S. (2014) 'A thematic analysis of preferences of young people using online support to discuss suicidal ideation', *International Journal of Transactional Analsysis Research*, 5(1): 3–8.

Follingstad, D.R. and Rogers, M.J. (2014) 'The nature and prevalence of partner psychological abuse in a national sample of adults', *Violence and Victims*, 29(1): 3–23.

Fox, R. and Cooper, M. (1998) 'The effects of suicide on the private practitioner: A professional and personal perspective', *Clinical Social Work Journal*, 26: 143–57.

Gardner, F. (2001) *Self-Harm: A Psychotherapeutic Approach*. London: Routledge.

Gaston, L., Thompson, L., Gallager, D., Cournoyer, L.G. and Gagnon, R. (1998) 'Alliance, technique and their interactions in predicting outcome of behavioural, cognitive and brief dynamic therapy', *Psychotherapy Research*, 8: 190–209.

Gilbert, P.R. (2007) *Psychotherapy and Counselling for Depression* (3rd edn). London: Sage.

Gray, A. (1994) *The Therapeutic Frame*. London: Routledge.

Hersh, J.B. (1985) 'Interviewing college students in crisis', *Journal of Counselling and Development*, 63: 286–9.

Hess, A.K. (ed.) (1980) *Psychotherapy Supervision: Theory, Research and Practice*. London: Wiley.

HM Government (2013) *Working Together to Safeguard Children*. London: Department of Education/Crown Publishing.

Hovarth, A.O. and Bedi, R.P. (2002) 'The Alliance', in J.C. Norcross (ed.), *Psychotherapy Relationships that Work: Therapist Contributions and Responsiveness to Patients*. New York: Oxford University Press. pp. 37–69.

Inskipp, F. and Proctor, B. (2001) *Becoming a Supervisor*. Twickenham: Cascade.

Jenkins, P. (2013) *Counselling, Psychotherapy and the Law*. London: Sage.

Jospeh, S. and Worsley, R. (2005) *Person-Centred Psychopathology: A Positive Psychology of Mental Health*. Ross-on-Wye: PCCS Books.

Lambert, M. (ed.) (2013) *Bergin and Garfield's Handbook of Psychotherapy and Behavior Change*. Chichester: Wiley.

Larcombe, A. (2008) 'Self-care in counselling', in W. Dryden and A. Reeves (eds), *Key Issues for Counselling in Action* (2nd edn). London: Sage. pp. 283–97.

Leach, C., Lucock, M., Barkham, M. and Noble, R. (2005) 'Assessing risk and emotional disturbance using the CORE-OM and HoNOS outcome measures at the interface between primary and secondary mental health care', *Psychiatric Bulletin*, 29: 419–22.

Leenaars, A.A. (2004) *Psychotherapy with Suicidal People: A Person-Centred Approach*. Chichester: Wiley.

Lemma, A. (1996) *Introduction to Psychopathology*. London: Sage.

Lord Chancellor's Department (1997) *Who Decides? Making Decisions on Behalf of Mentally Incapacitated Adults*. Available at: www.dca. gov.uk/menincap/meninfr.htm (accessed 30 May 2014).

Lord Chancellor's Department (1999) *Making Decisions: The Government's Proposals for Making Decisions on Behalf of Mentally Incapacitated Adults*. Available at: http://webarchive.national archives.gov.uk/+/www.dca.gov.uk/family/mdecisions/indexfr.htm (accessed 30 May 2014).

Maslow, A.H. (1943) 'A theory of human motivation', *Psychological Review*, 50(4): 370–96.

Masson, J.M. (1988) *Against Therapy*. London: Flamingo.

Mattinson, J. (1975) *The Reflection Process in Casework Supervision*. London: Institute of Marital Studies.

Miller, M.C., Jacobs, D.G. and Gutheil, T.G. (1998) 'Talisman or taboo: The controversy of the suicide-prevention contract', *Harvard Review of Psychiatry*, 6: 78–87.

Mitchels, B. and Bond, T. (2010) *Essential Law for Counsellors and Psychotherapists*. London: Sage.

Newhill, C. (2014) *Risk Assessment, Violent Clients and Practitioner Safety*. University of Pittsburgh Social Work Department. Available at: www.socialworkpodcast.com/Client%20Violence%20Workshop%20 Handout.pdf (accessed 29 May 2014).

Newnes, C. and Dunn, C. (1999) *This is Madness: A Critical Look at Psychiatry and the Future of Mental Health Services*. Ross-on-Wye: PCCS Books.

NICE (National Institute for Clinical and Health Excellence) (2004) *Eating Disorders: Core Interventions in the Treatment and Management of Anorexia Nervosa, Bulimia Nervosa and Related Eating Disorders*. Clinical Guidance 9. London: NICE.

NICE (National Institute for Clinical and Health Excellence) (2011) *Self-Harm: Longer-Term Management (NICE Clinical Guidance 133)*. Manchester: NICE.

Niolon, R. (2006) *Dangerous Clients: Assessment and Work Resources for Students and Professionals*. Available at: www.psychpage.com/ learning/library/counseling/danger.htm (accessed 29 May 2014).

NSPCC (2014a) *Emotional Abuse*. Available at: www.nspcc.org.uk/ Inform/research/briefings/emotionalabuse_wda48215.html (accessed 8 August 2014).

NSPCC (2014b) *Briefings and Factsheets: Short Introductions to Child Protection, Child Abuse and Safeguarding Topics.* Available at: www. nspcc.org.uk/Inform/research/briefings/briefings_wda48208.html (accessed 30 May 2014).

Oxford English Dictionary (2014) Online database: www.oed.com (accessed 7 May 2014).

Pompili, M., Manchinelli, I. and Tatarelli, R (2002a) 'Dealing with patient suicide', *Minerva Psichiatrica*, 43: 181–6.

Pompili, M., Manchinelli, I. and Tatarelli, R. (2002b) 'Beyond the therapeutic challenge: On countertransference problems with the patient at risk of commiting suicide', *Psichiatria a Psicoterapia Analitica*, 21: 217–28.

Quinsey, V.L., Harris, G.T., Rice, M.E. and Cormier, C.A. (1998) *Violent Offenders: Appraising and Managing Risk.* Washington, DC: American Psychological Association.

Reeves, A. and Mintz, R. (2001) 'Counsellors' experiences of working with suicidal clients: An exploratory study', *Counselling and Psychotherapy Research*, 1(3): 172–6.

Reeves, A., Bowl, R., Wheeler, S. and Guthrie, E. (2004) 'The hardest words: Exploring the dialogue of suicide in the counselling process – a discourse analysis', *Counselling and Psychotherapy Research*, 4(1): 62–71.

Reeves, A. and Coldridge, E. (2007) 'A question of balance: Using CORE-OM to assess suicide risk', *Journal of the Association for University and College Counsellors*, May.

Reeves, A. (2010) *Counselling Suicidal Clients.* London: Sage.

Reeves, A. (2013a) *Challenges in Counselling: Self-Harm.* London: Hodder Education.

Reeves, A. (2013b) *An Introduction to Counselling and Psychotherapy: From Theory to Practice.* London: Sage.

Roth, A. and Fonagy, P. (2005) *What Works for Whom? A Critical Review of Psychotherapy Research* (2nd edn). London: The Guilford Press.

Royal College of Psychiatrists (2010) *Self-Harm, Suicide and Risk: Helping People Who Self-Harm.* London: Royal College of Psychiatrists College Report CR158.

Ruddell, P. and Curwen, B. (2008) 'Understanding suicidal ideation and assessing for risk', in S. Palmer (ed.), *Suicide: Strategies and Interventions for Reduction and Prevention.* London: Routledge. pp. 84–99.

Russello, A. (2008) *Recognising Mental Health and Mental Health Problems: G7 Information Sheet.* Lutterworth: BACP.

Sanders, P. (2007) 'Decoupling psychological therapies from the medical model', *Therapy Today*, 18(9): 8–10.

Shneidman, E. (1996) *The Suicidal Mind.* Oxford: Oxford University Press.

Sills, C. (ed.) (2006) *Contracts in Counselling and Psychotherapy* (2nd edn). London: Sage.

Sommerbeck, L. (2003) *The Client-Centred Therapist in Psychiatric Contexts: A Therapists' Guide to the Psychiatric Landscape and its Inhabitants.* Ross-on-Wye: PCCS Books.

Spinelli, E. (2006) *Demystifying Therapy.* Ross-on-Wye: PCCS Books.

Topor, A., Andersson, G., Denhov, A., Holmqvist, S., Mattsson, E., Stefansson, C. and Bülow, P. (2013) 'Psychosis and poverty: Coping with poverty and severe mental illness in everyday life', *Psychosis: Psychological, Social and Integrative Approaches,* 6(2): 117–27.

Tunick, R.A., Mednick, L. and Conroy, C. (2011) 'A snapshot of child psychologists' social media activity: Professional and ethical practice implications and recommendations', *Professional Psychology: Research and Practice,* 42(6): 440–7.

Turp, M. (2002) *Hidden Self-Harm: Narratives from Psychotherapy.* London: Jessica Kingsley.

van Rijn, B. (2015) *Assessment and Case Formulation: Essential Issues in Counselling and Psychotherapy.* London: Sage.

Vicarious Trauma Institute (2014) *Vicarious Trauma: What is It?* Available at: www.vicarioustrauma.com/whatis.html (accessed 5 May 2014).

Walker, D.C. and Murray, A.D. (2014) 'Body checking and avoidance in men: Current findings and future directions', in L. Cohn and R. Lemberg (eds), *Current Findings on Males with Eating Disorders.* pp. 135–47.

Winter, D., Bradshaw, S., Bunn, F. and Wellsted, D. (2009) *Counselling and Psychotherapy for the Prevention of Suicide: A Systematic Review of the Evidence.* Lutterworth: BACP.

World Health Organization (1992) *The ICD-10 Classification of Mental and Behavioural Disorders: Clinical Descriptions and Diagnostic Guidelines.* Geneva: WHO.

World Health Organization (2014) Suicide Prevention (SUPRE). Available at: www.who.int/mental_health/prevention/suicide/suicideprevent/en/ (accessed 7 August 2014).

INDEX

Note: Page numbers in **bold** indicate a comprehensive coverage of the topic.

www.ingramcontent.com/pod-product-compliance
Lightning Source LLC
Chambersburg PA
CBHW060041030426
42334CB00019B/2433